The Beautiful Children of the Mekong
By Thomas Auer

Dedicated to my loving wife and family.

Thank you to Avalon Waterways, a member of the Globus Travel Company, and the fabulous crew of the Saigon. A special thank you to the amazing Cruise Director Phiem.

ISBN: 978-1-7362330-7-8 (hardcover)
ISBN: 978-1-7362330-8-5 (paperback)
Also available for Kindle

On an amazing trip to Cambodia in 2019, my wife and I spent a week on the Saigon, a small cruise ship run by Avalon Waterways. It was a wonderful way to explore the Mekong River Valley and to see and meet the people who live and work there.

One of the things that impressed me the most were the children. They were friendly, intelligent, engaging, and loved to have their pictures taken. Even though they lacked many of the comforts afforded to children in the U.S., they expressed a keen interest in the outside world and an appetite for learning. They were excited to meet our small group of outsiders and to welcome us into their surroundings. We saw them at play, at work, and at school.

They entertained us, smiled at us, and cooked for us. They exuded a sparkle in their eyes and a joyful expression on their faces. Their smiles were warm and sincere. Their interactions with their parents demonstrated a respectful and loving relationship. It was clear that their parents were proud of their children and gladly showed them off.

This photographic journal is intended to show the reader the wonders, the energy, and the beauty of the children of the Mekong River Vally in Cambodia. Enjoy!!!!

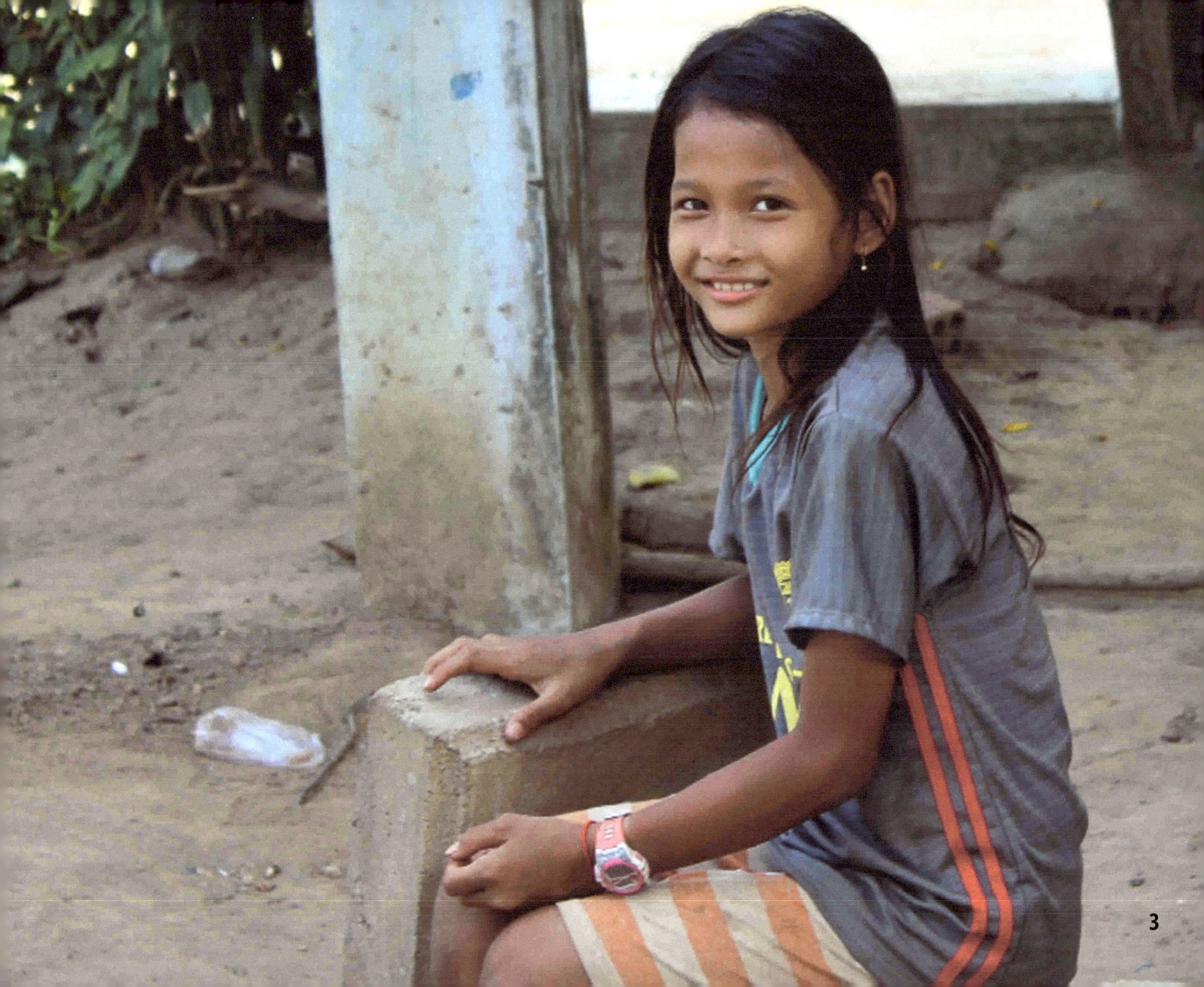

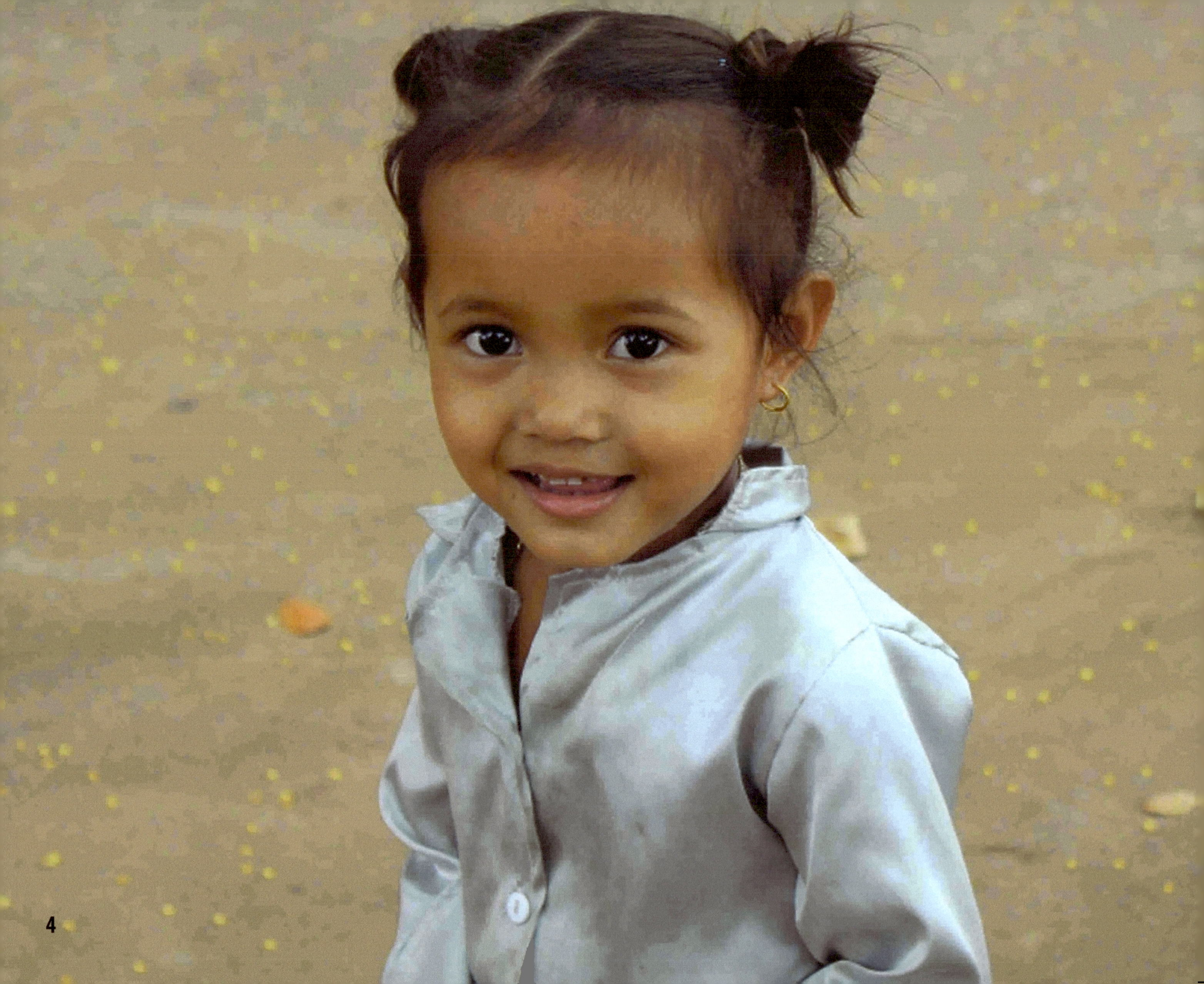

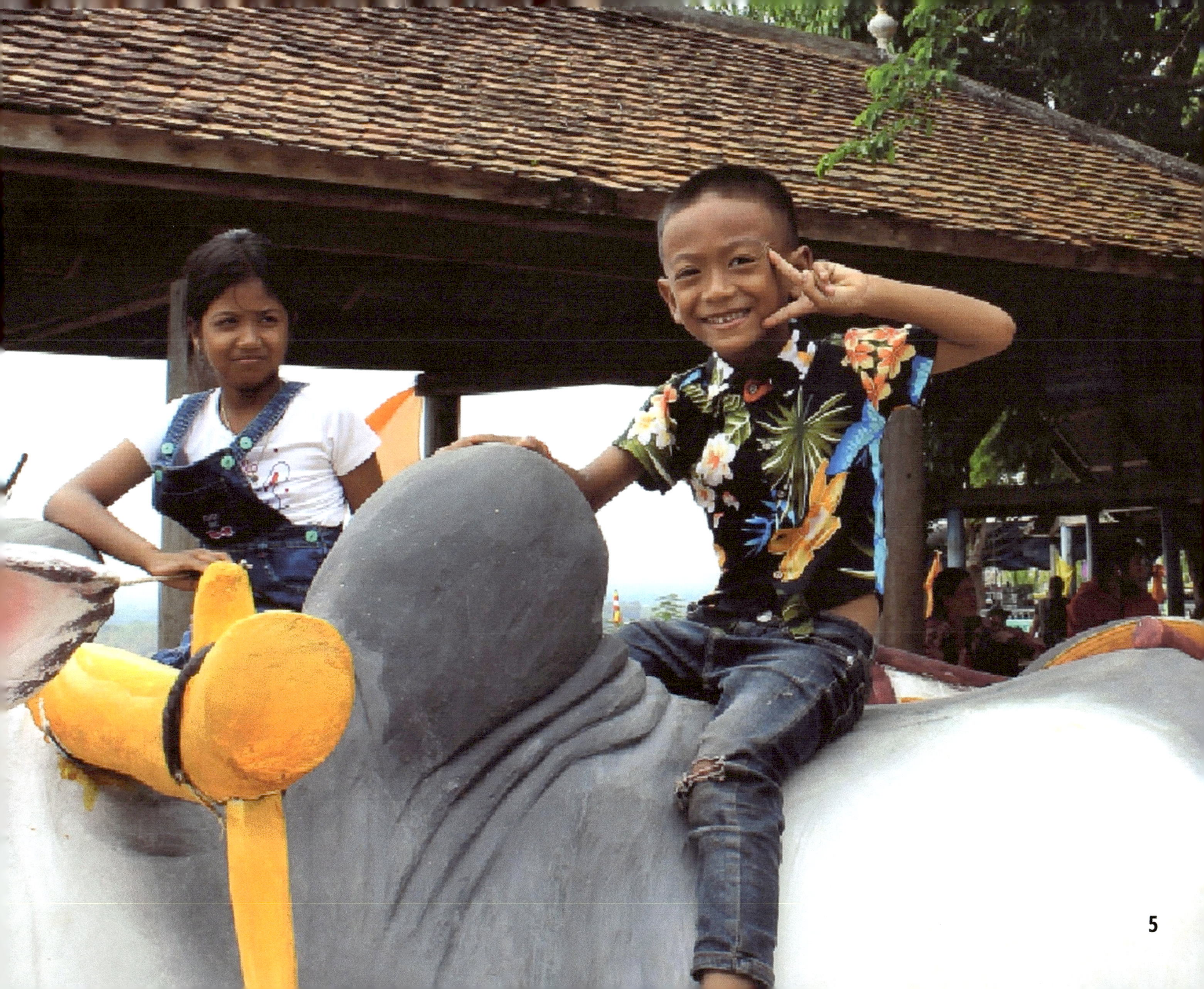

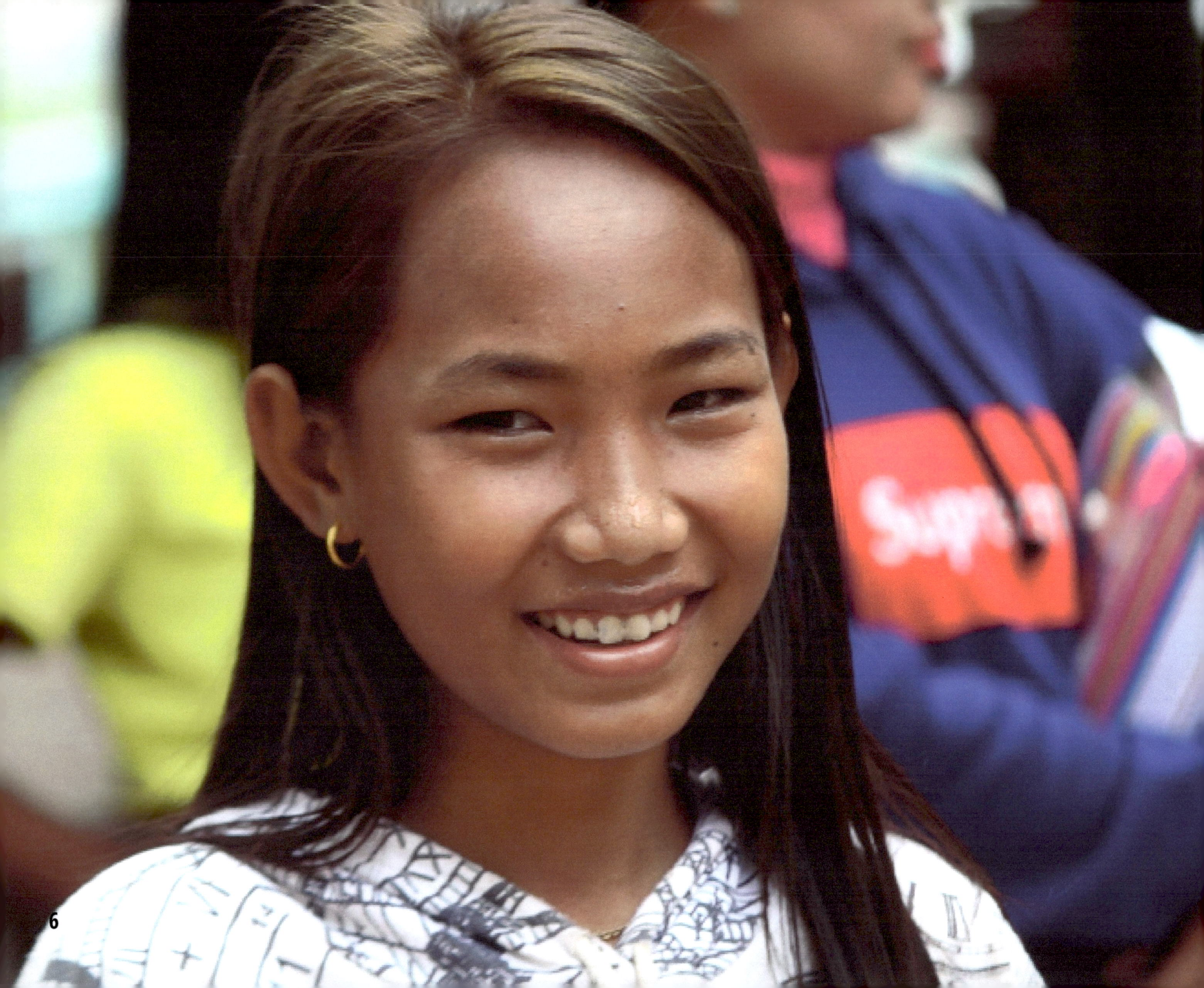

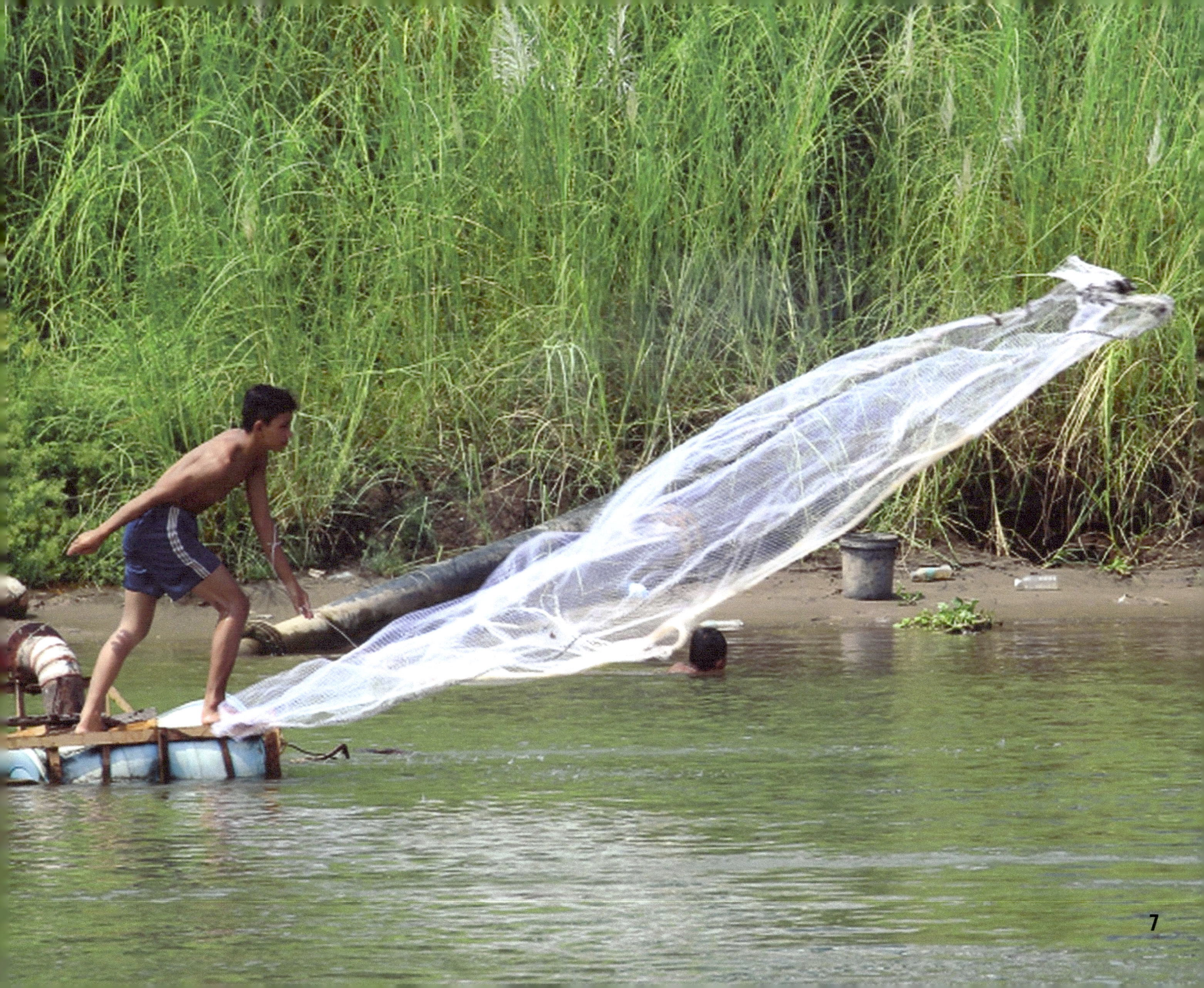

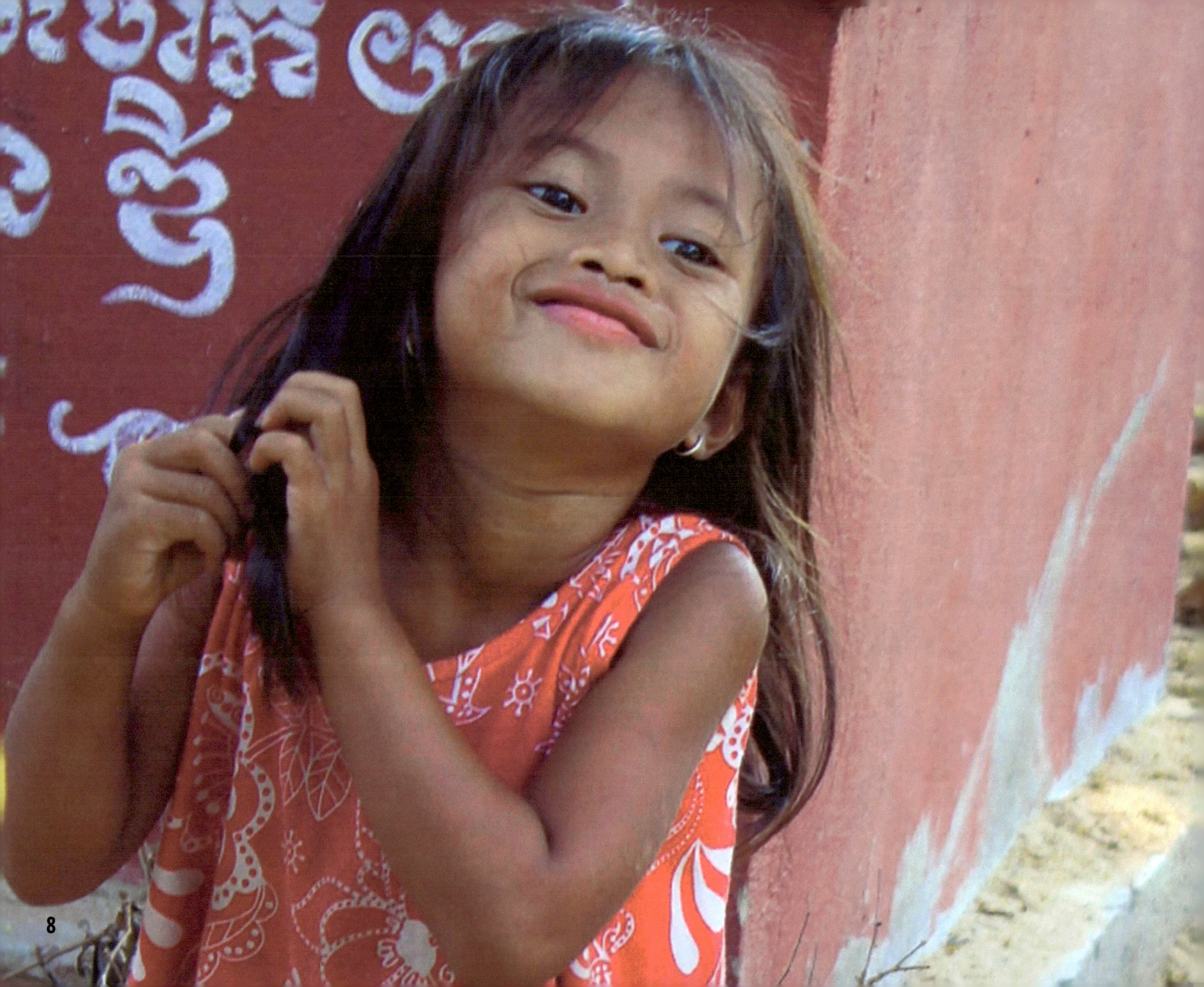

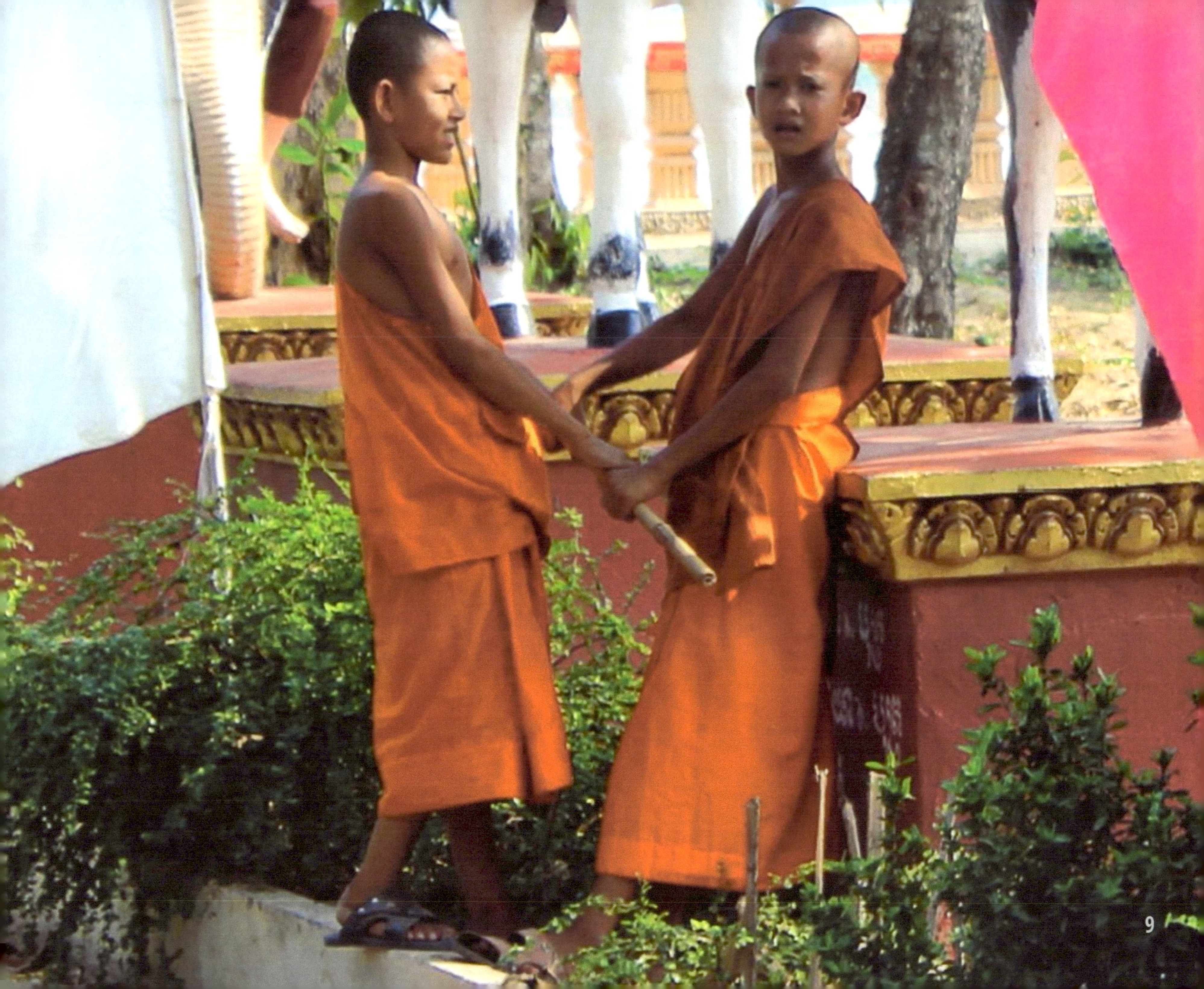

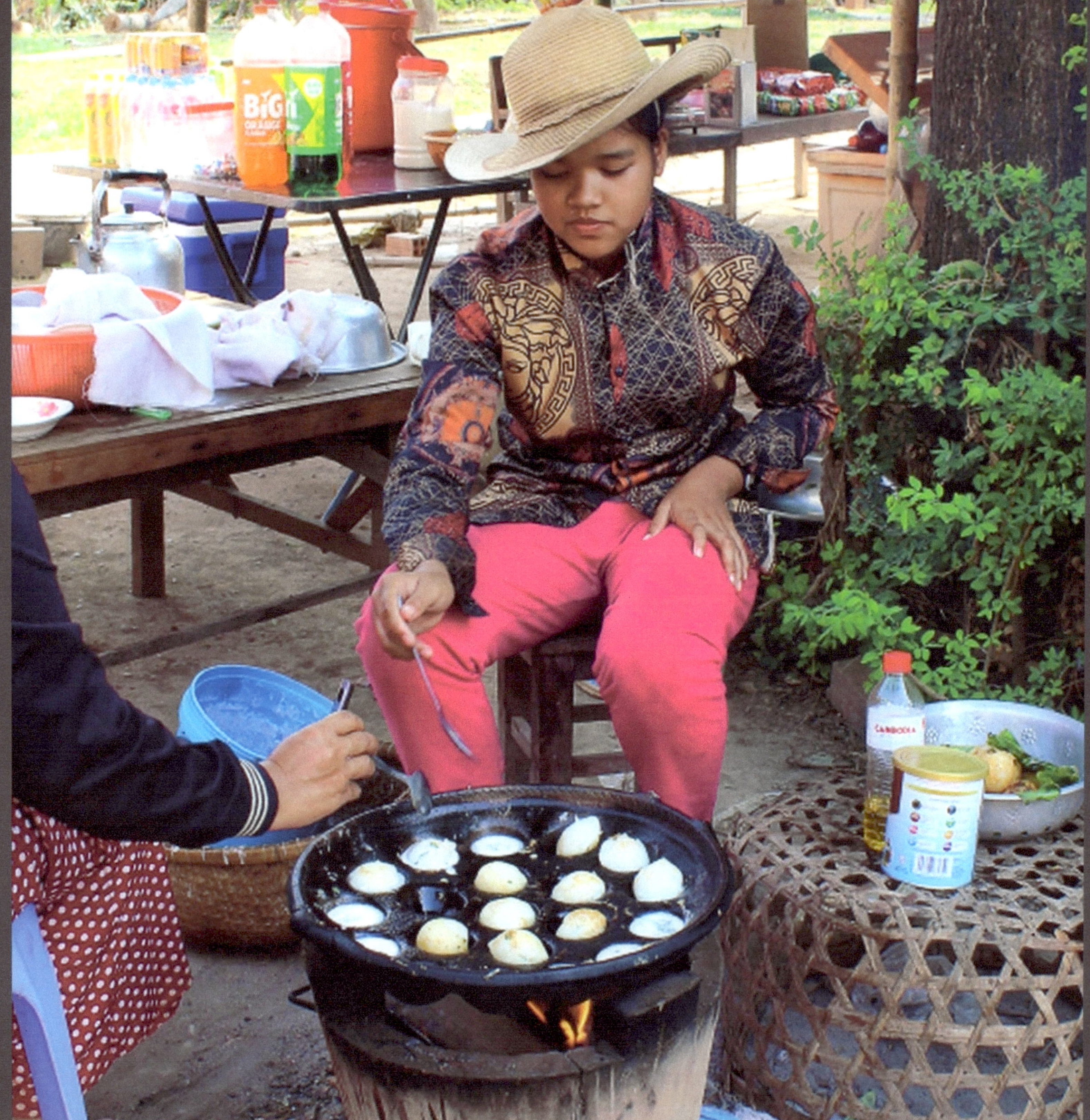

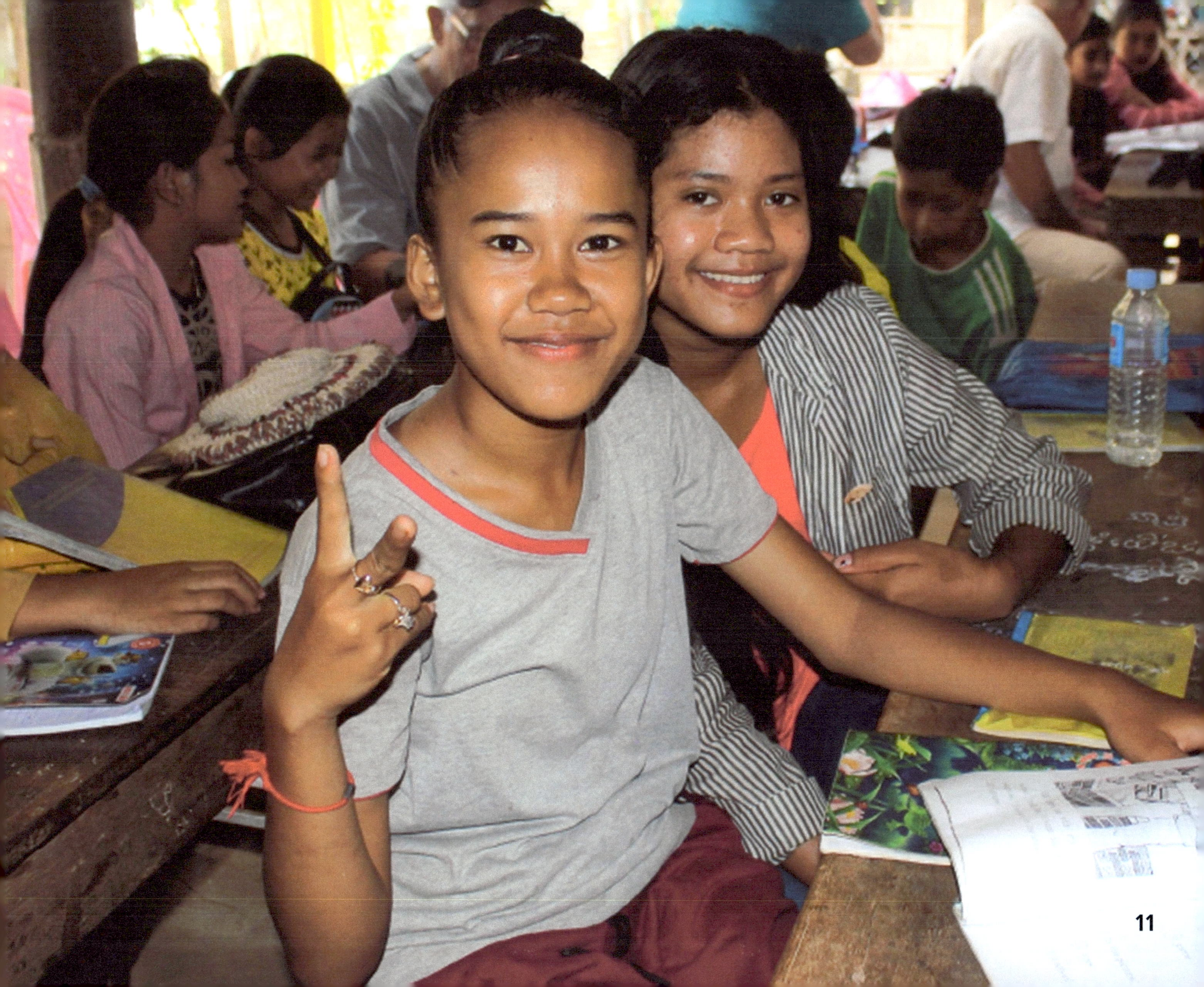

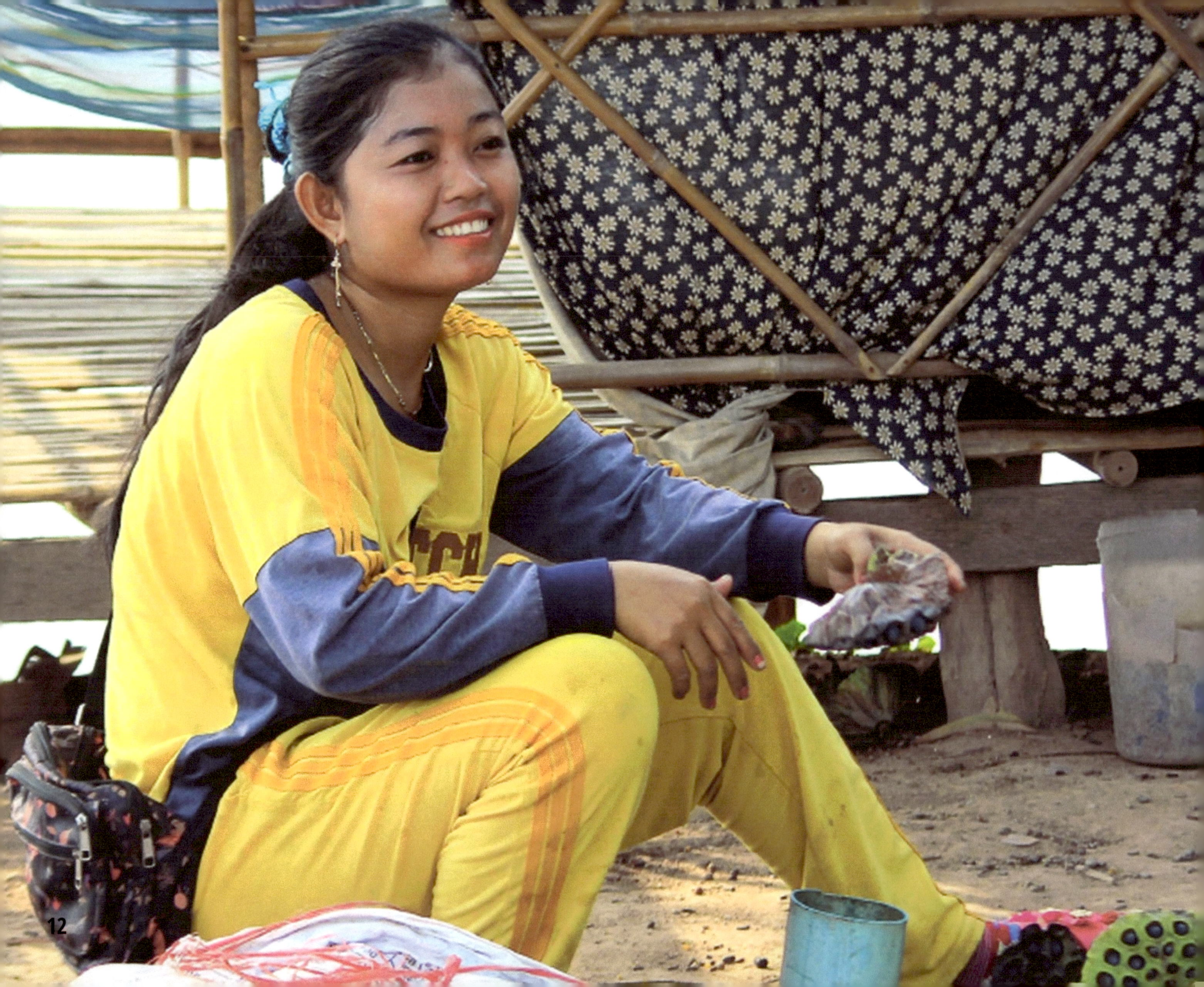

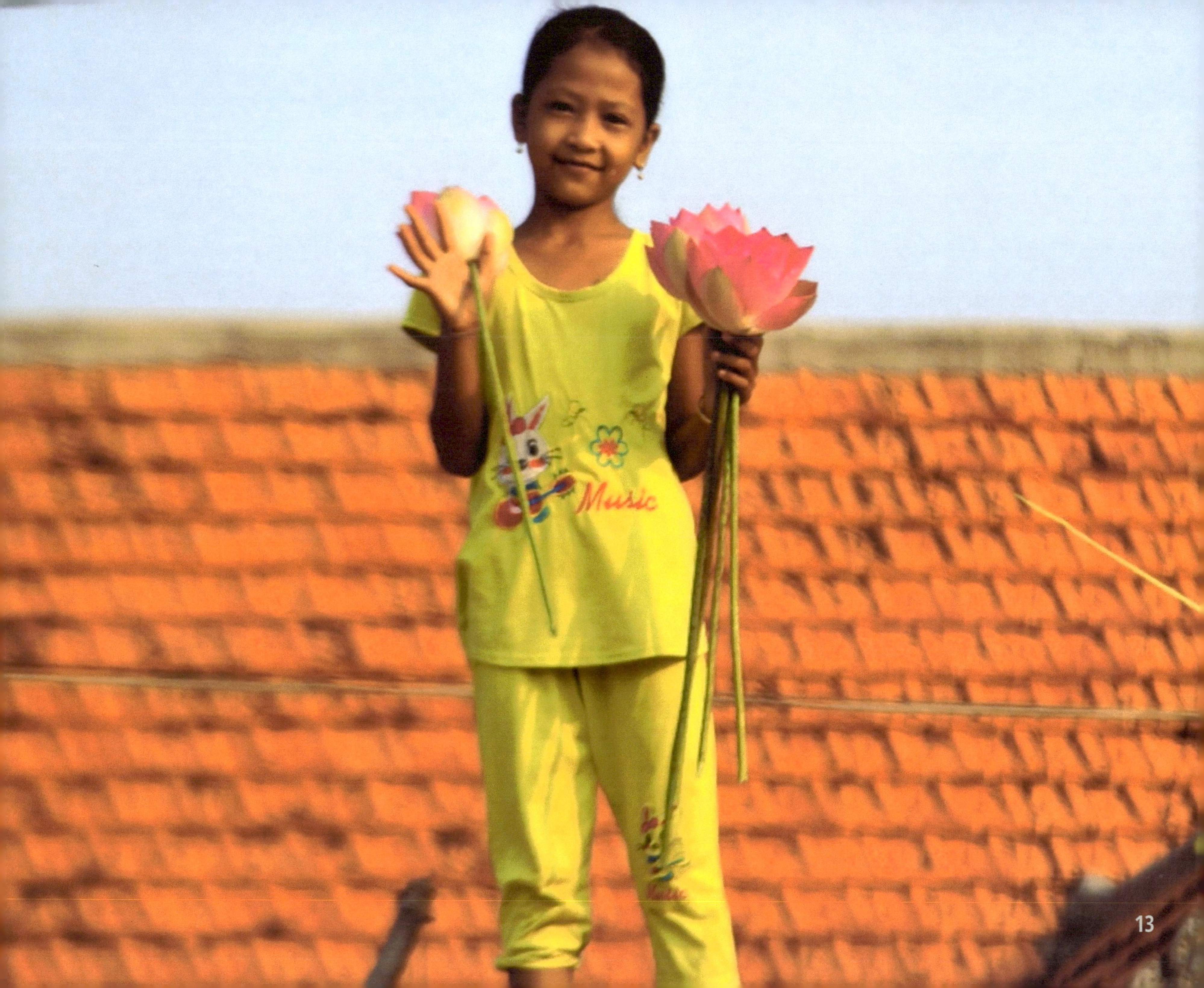

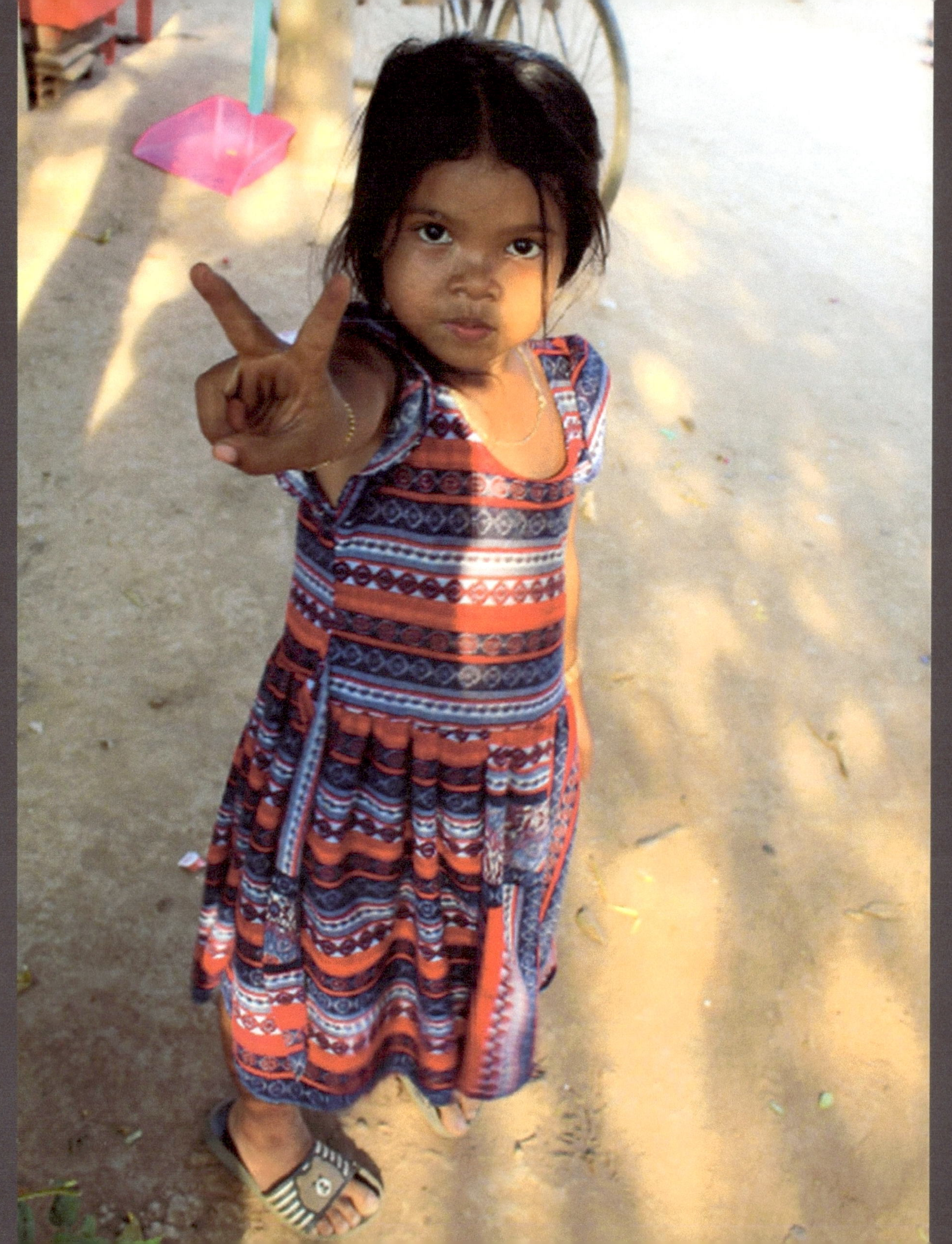

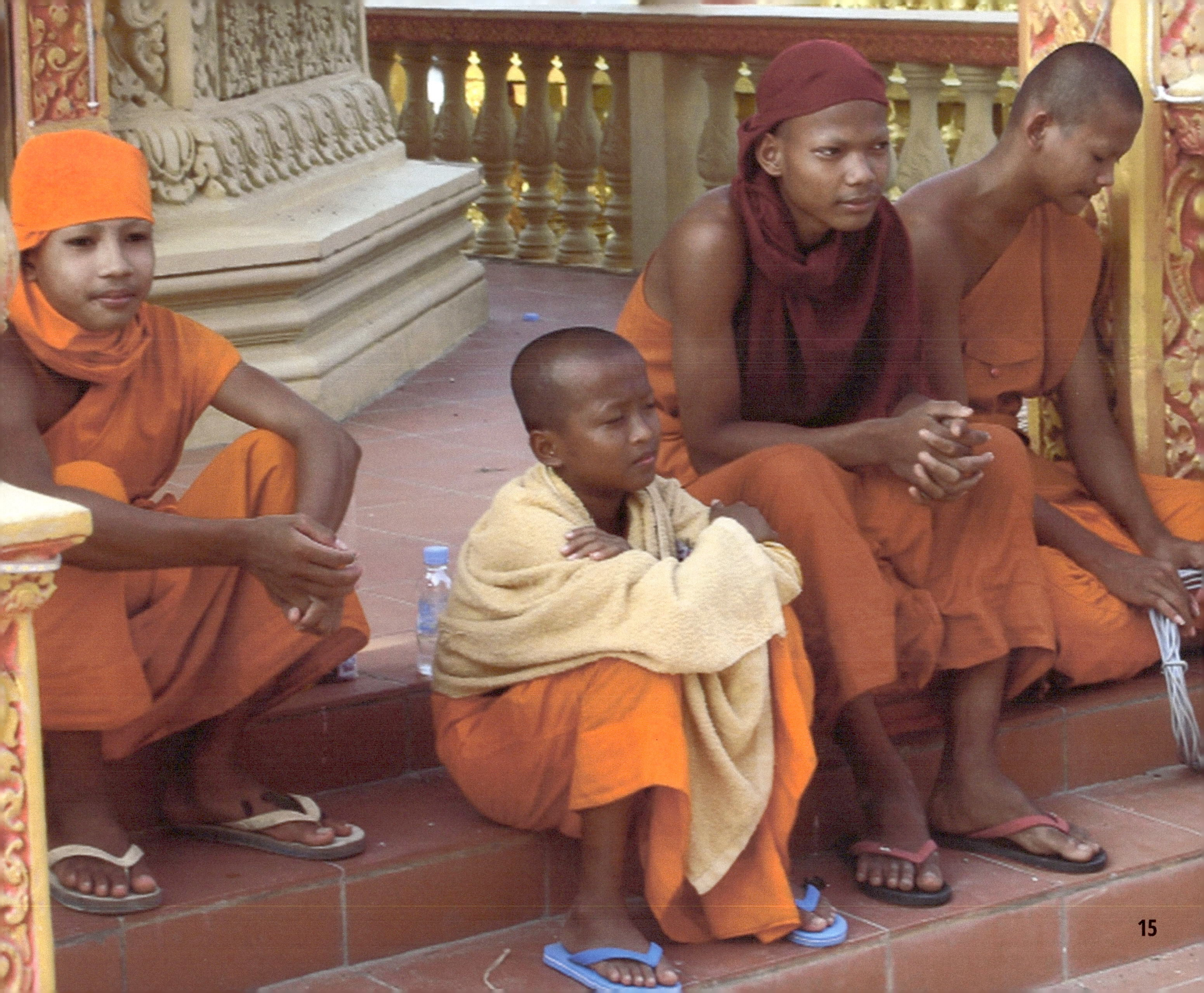

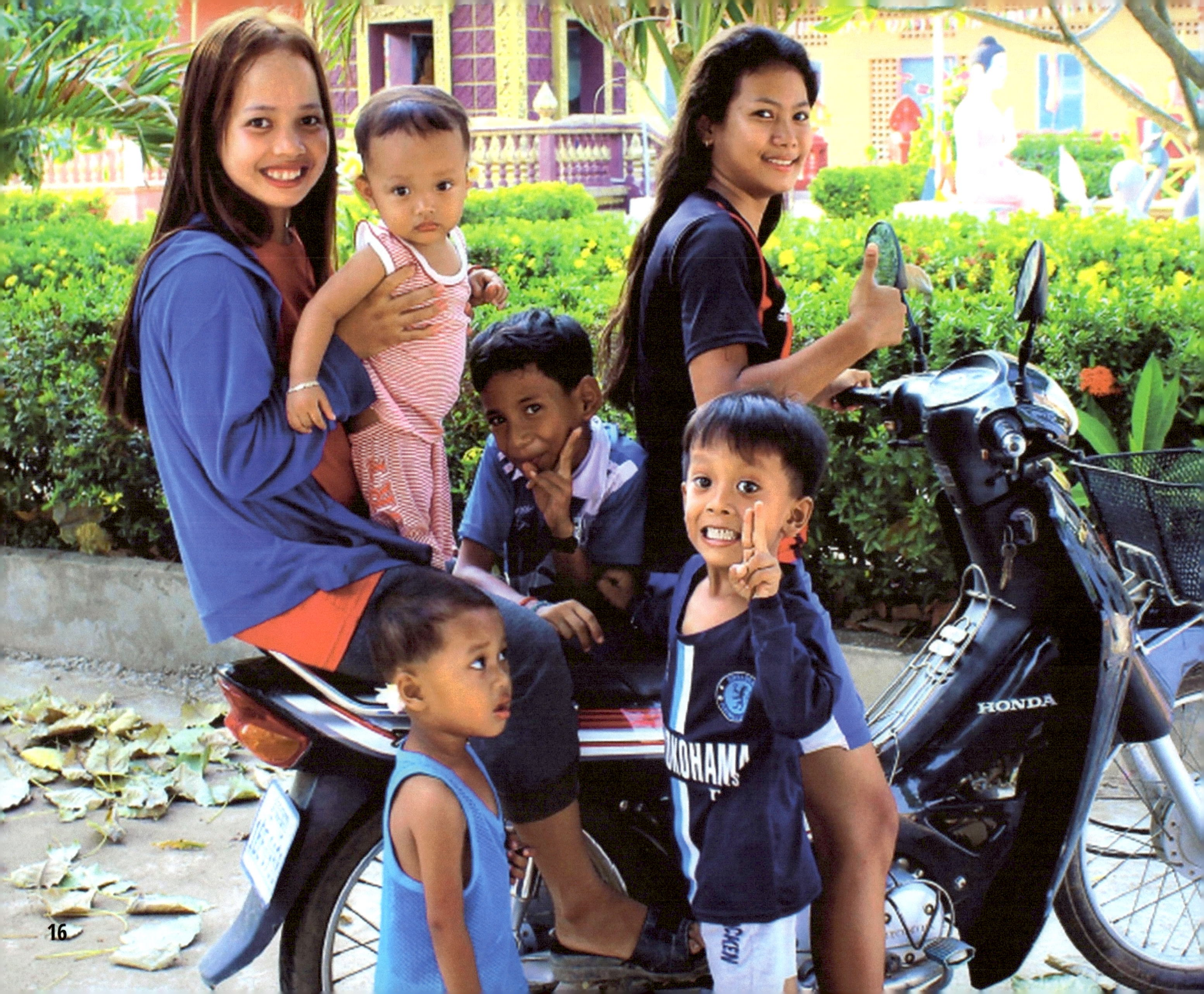

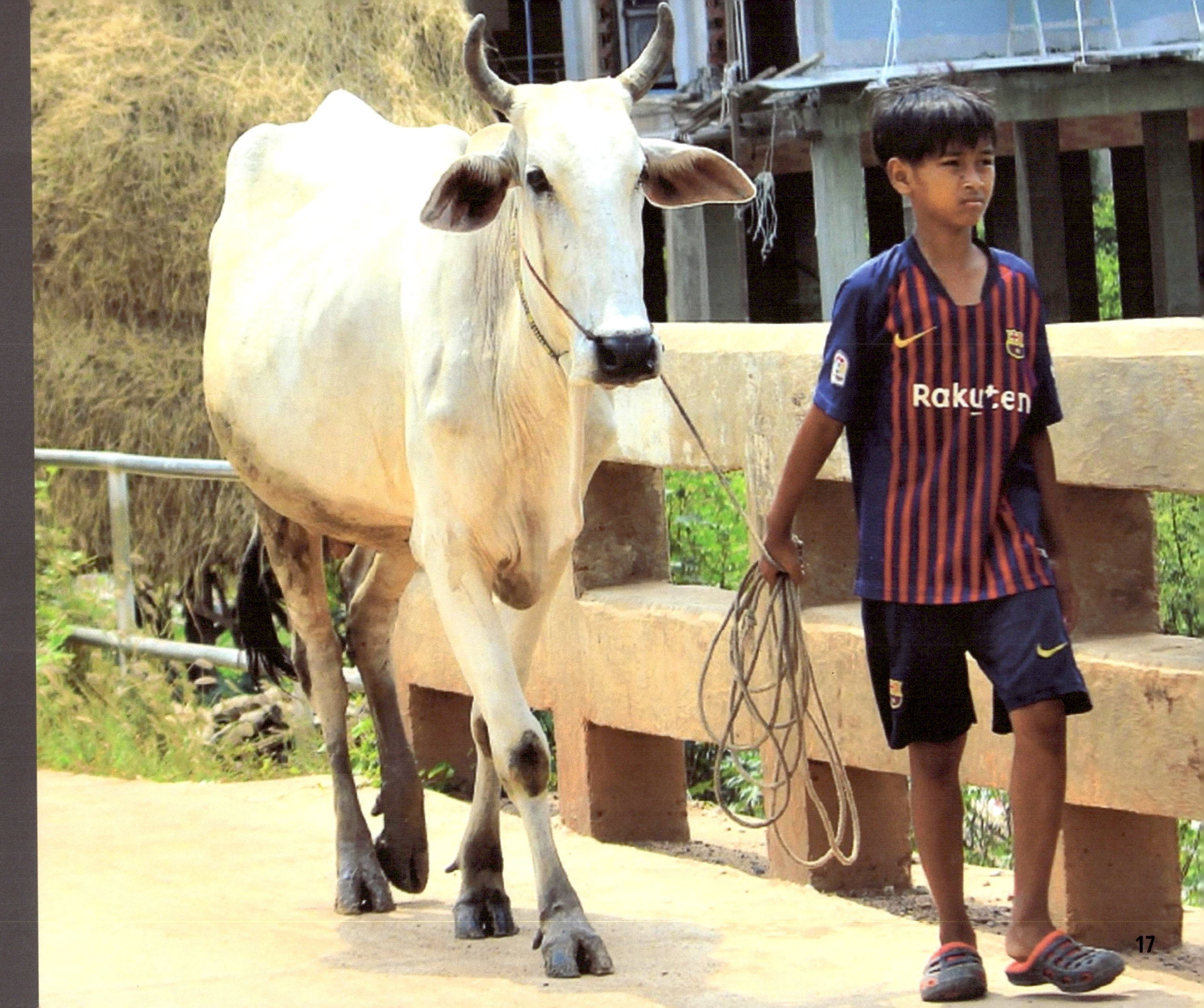

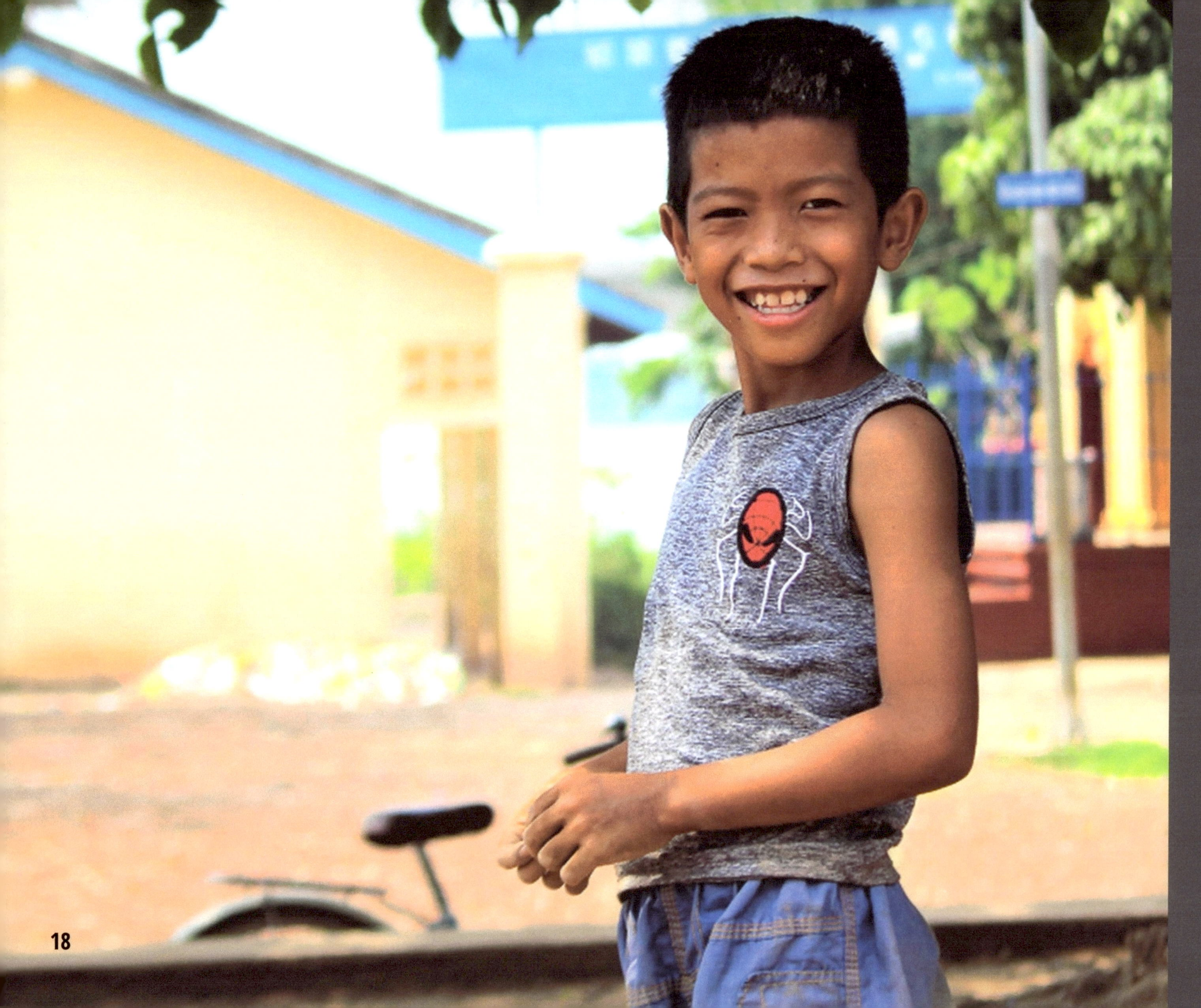

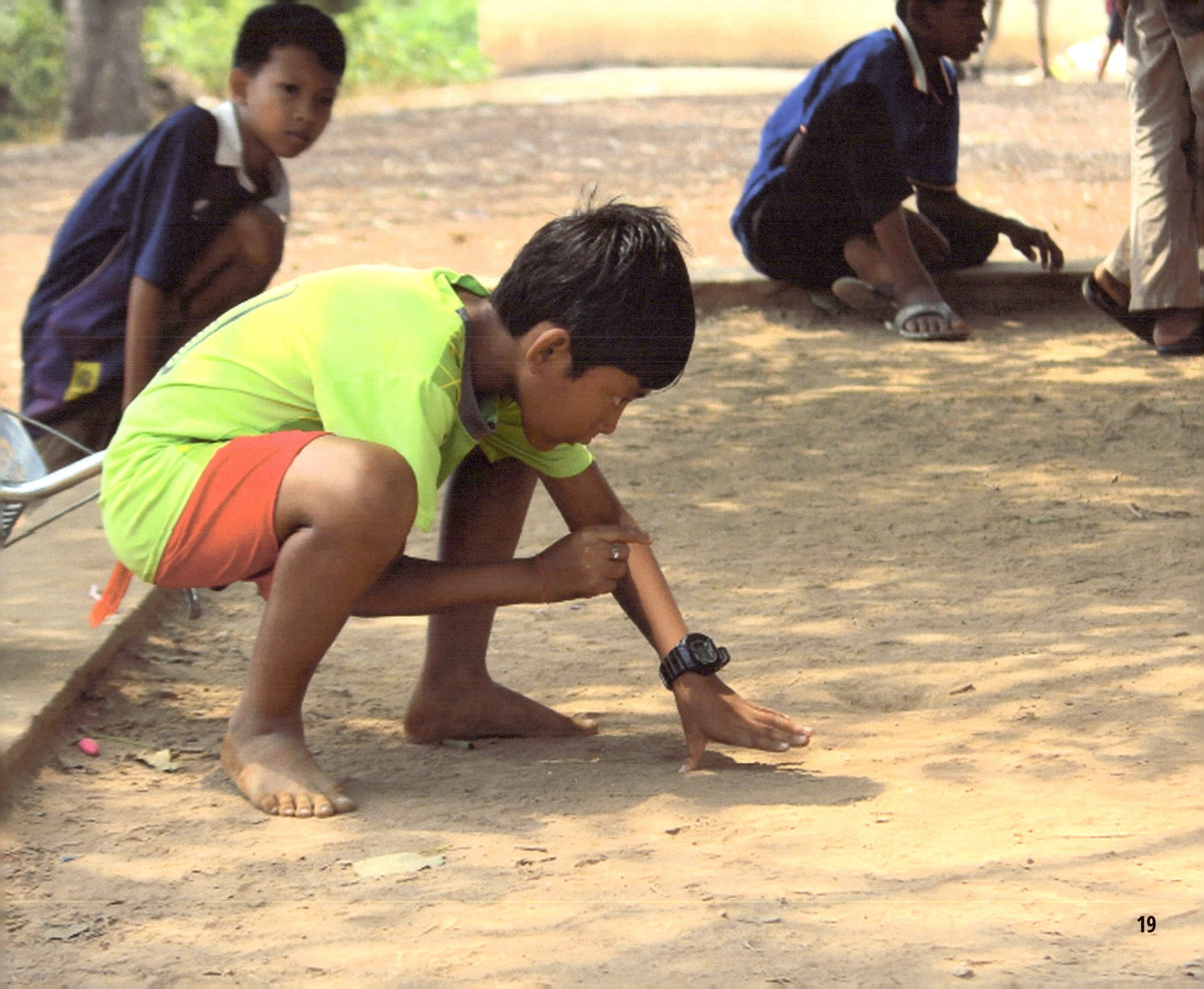

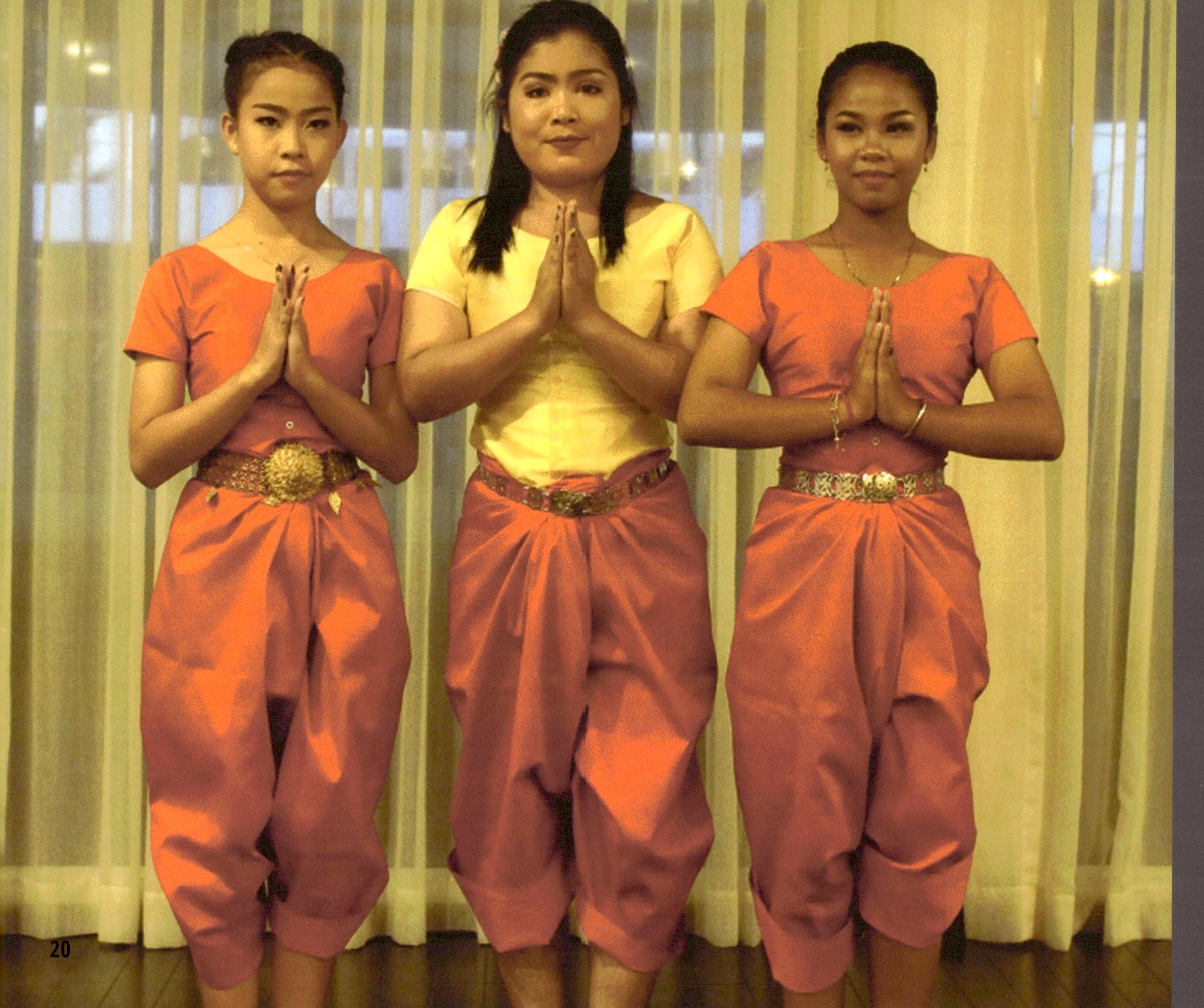

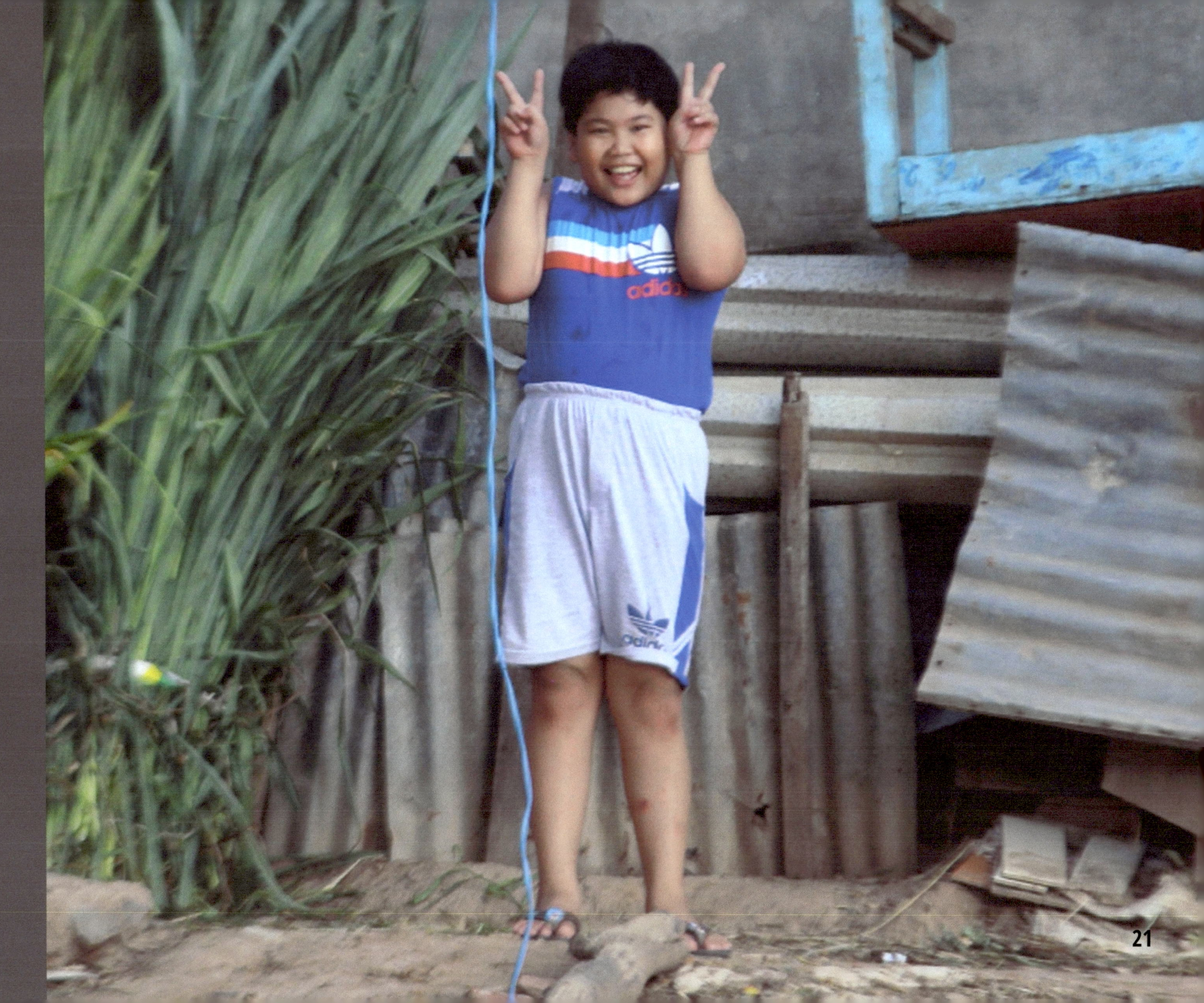

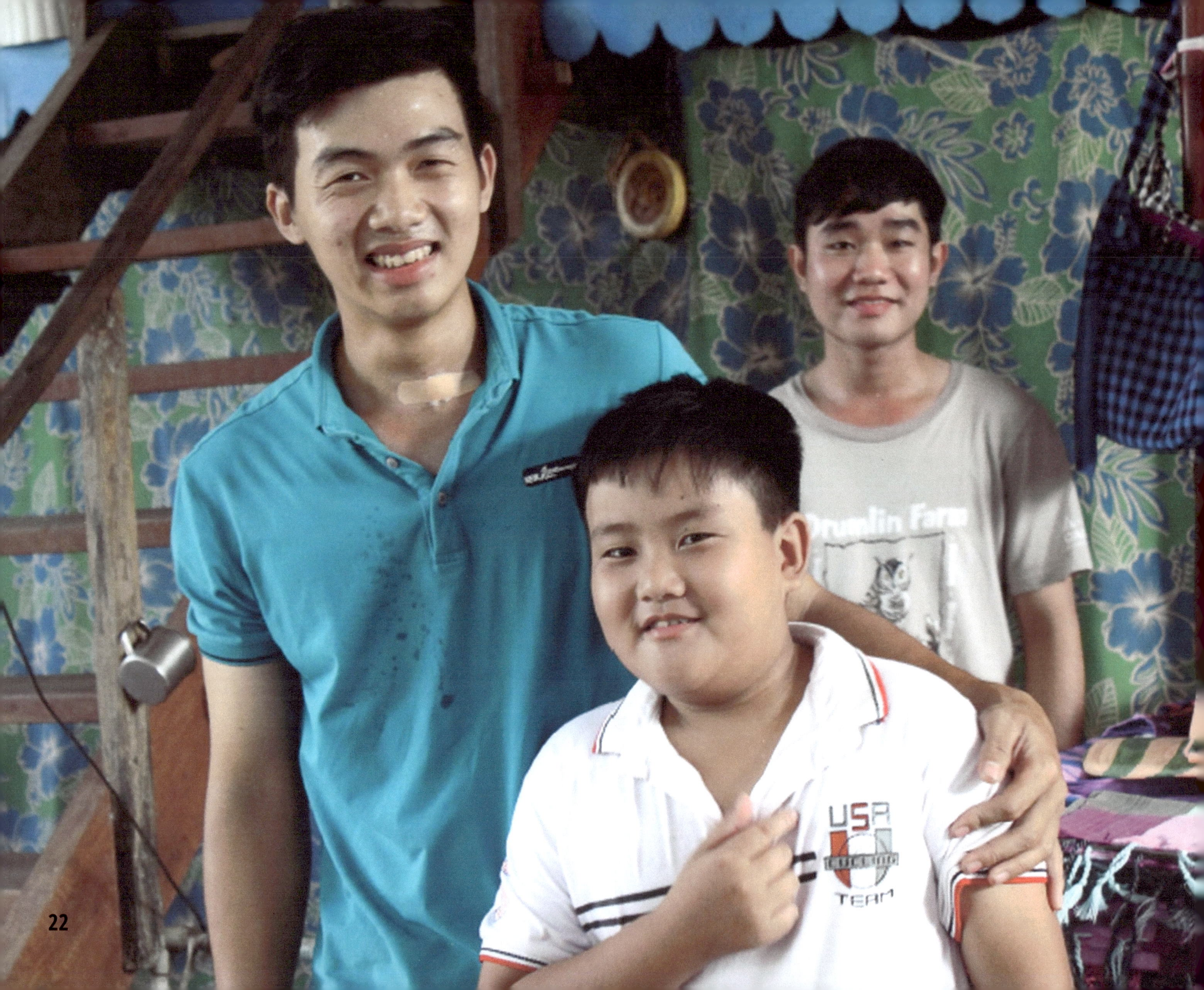

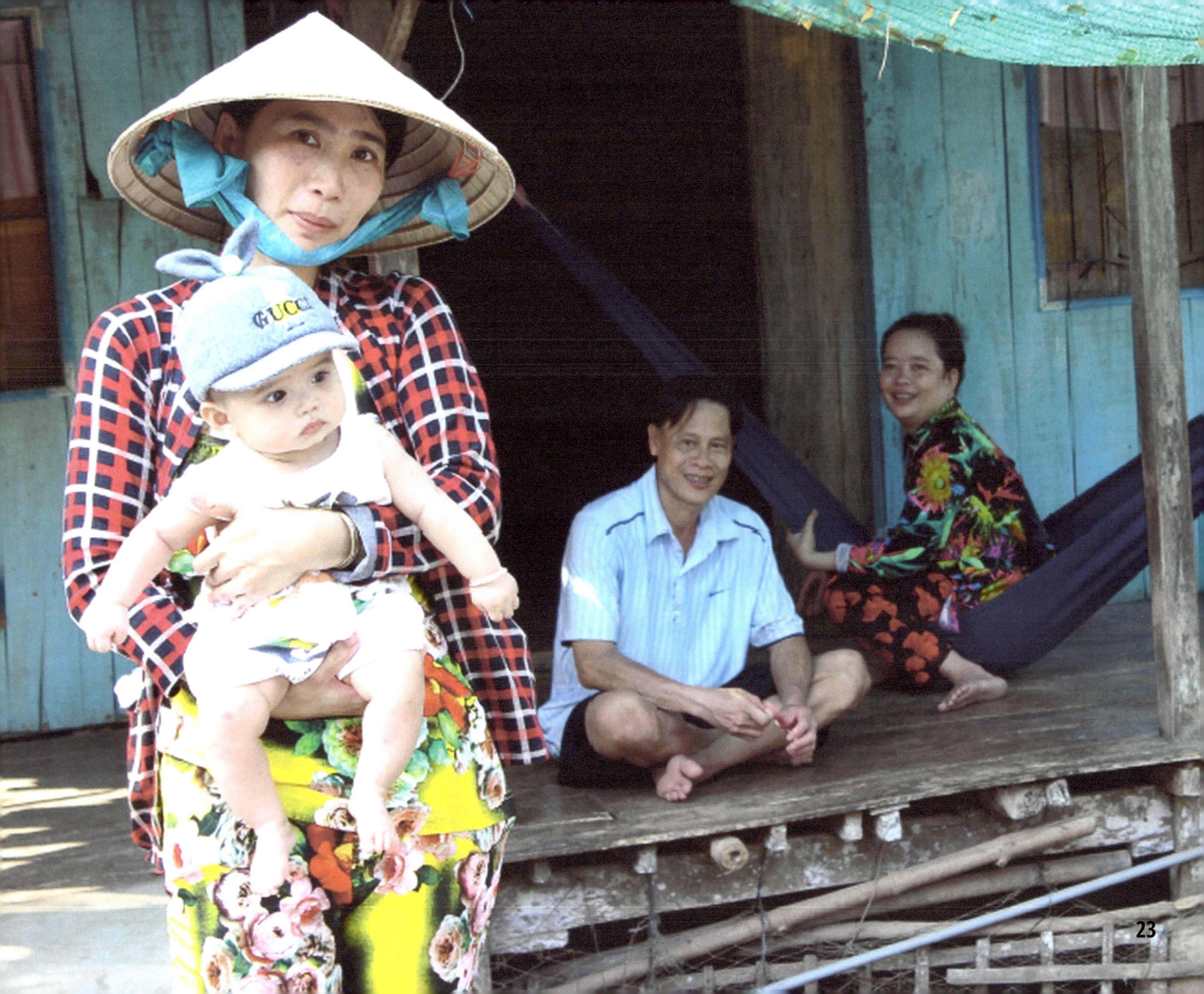

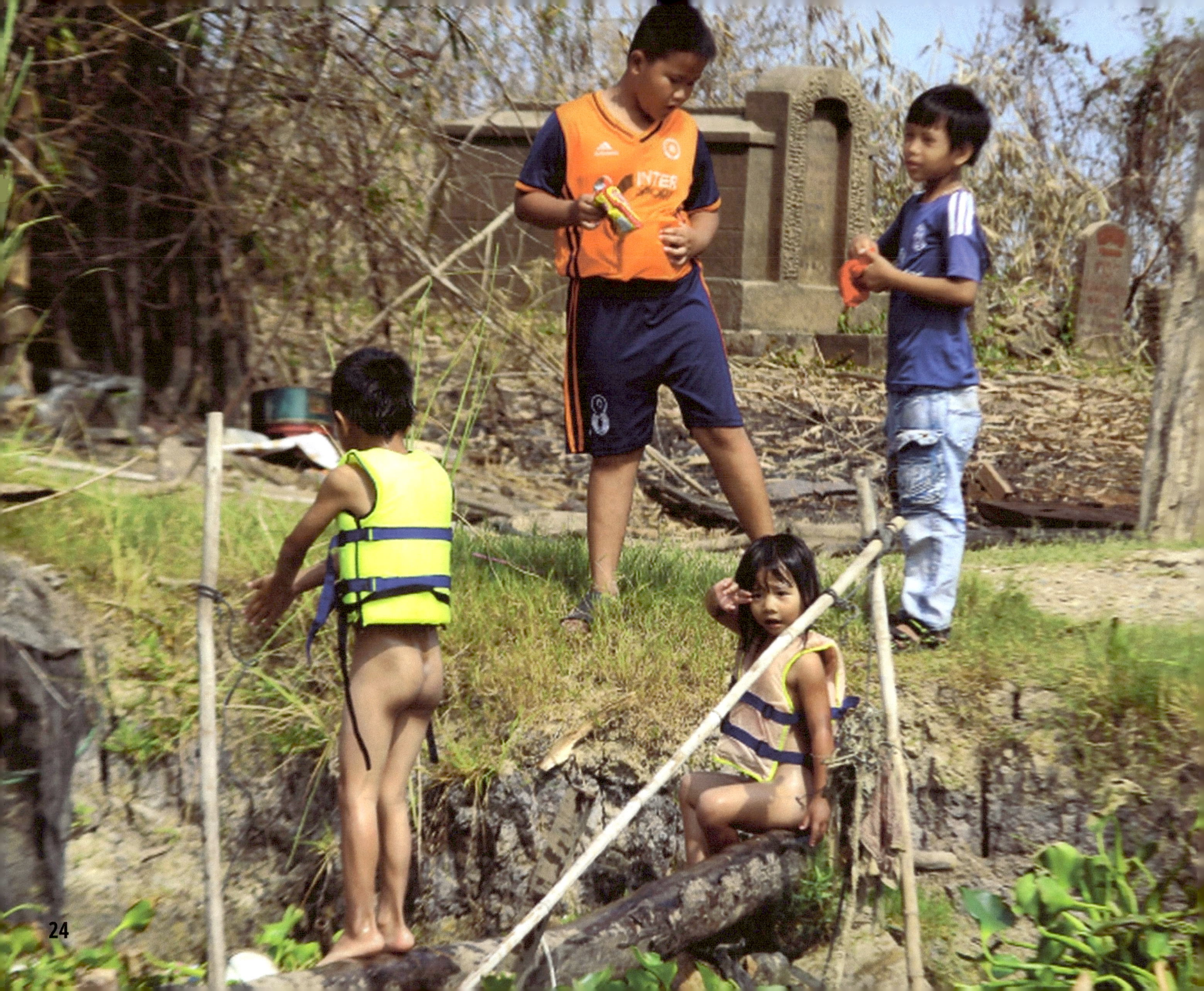

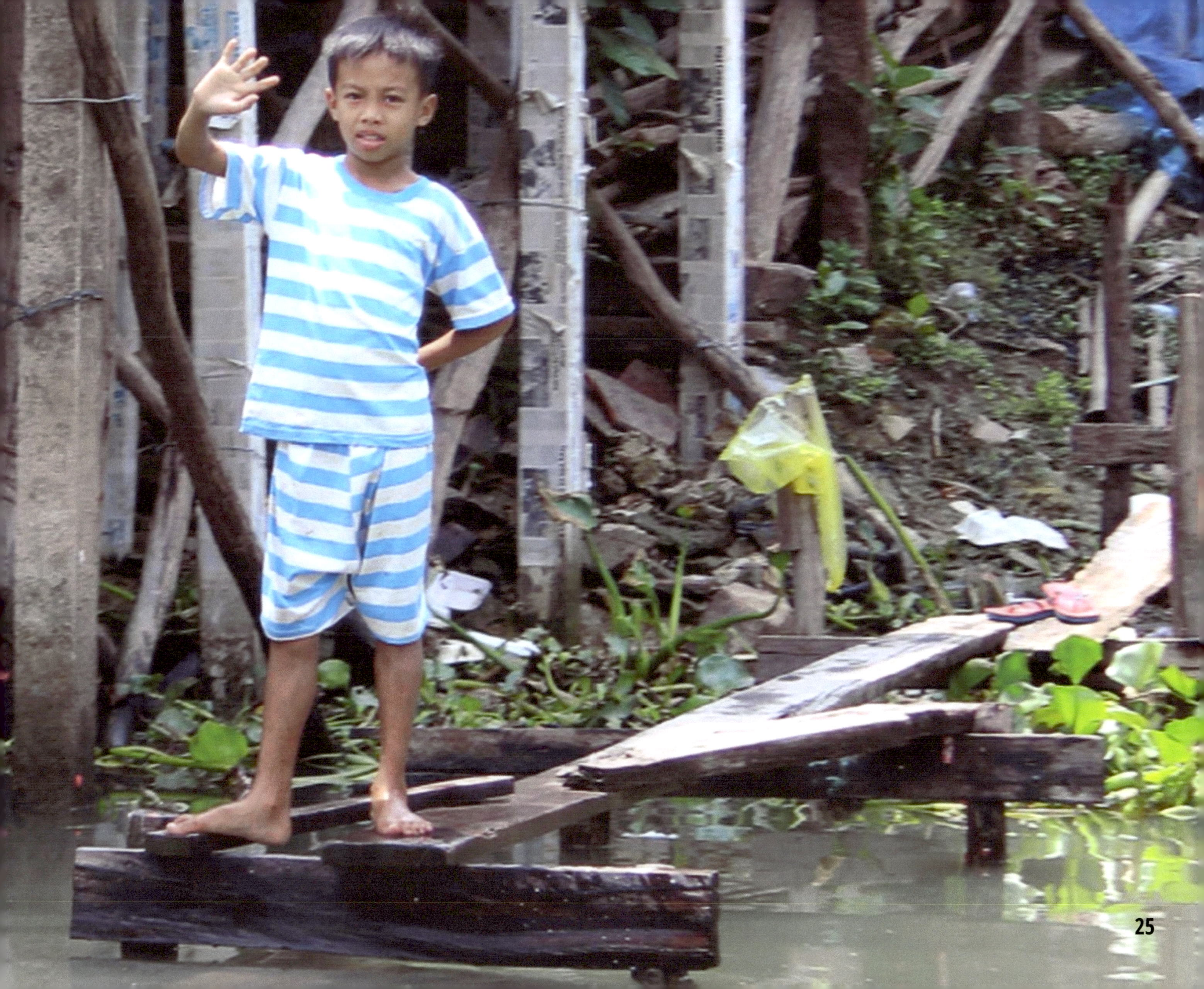

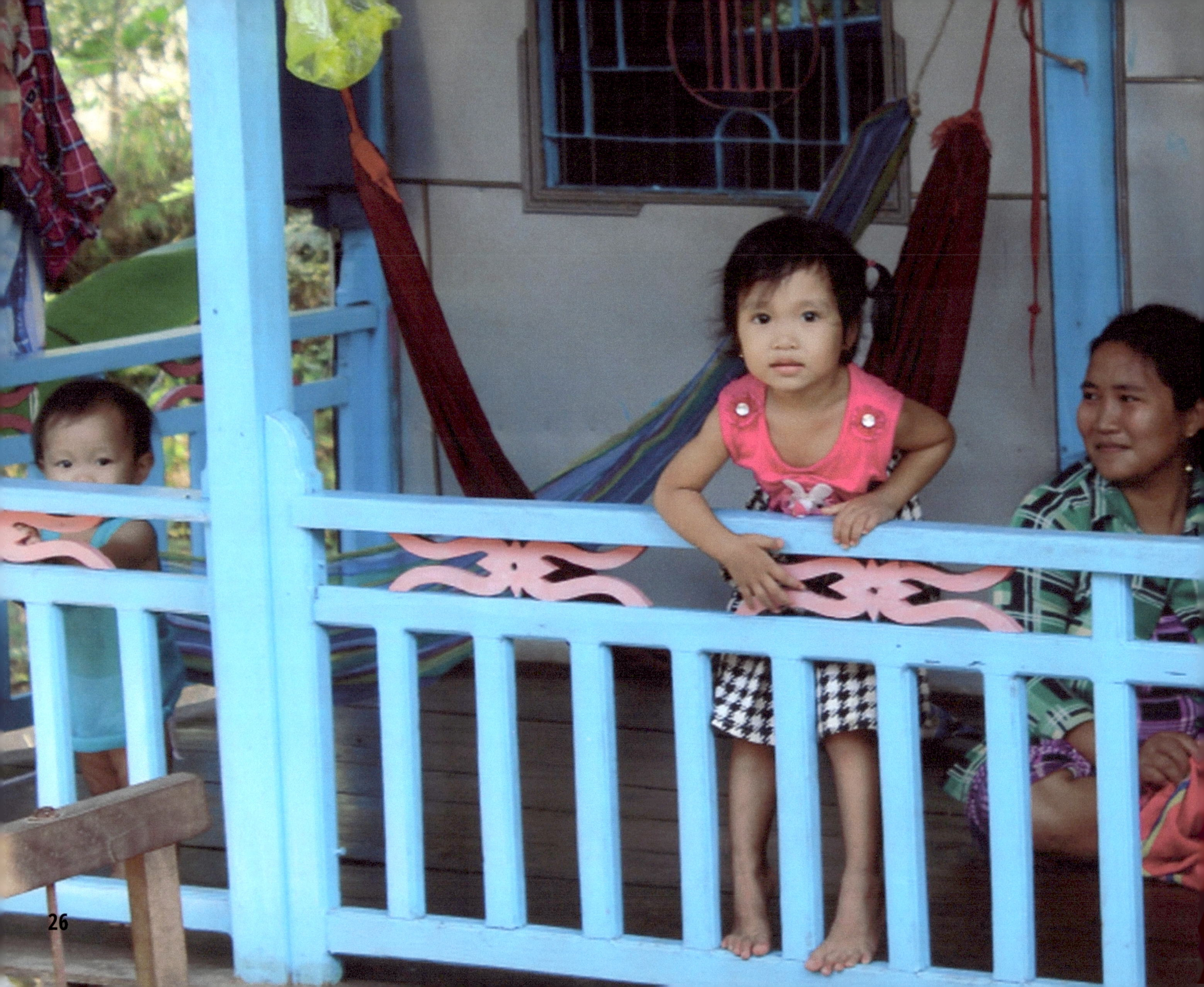

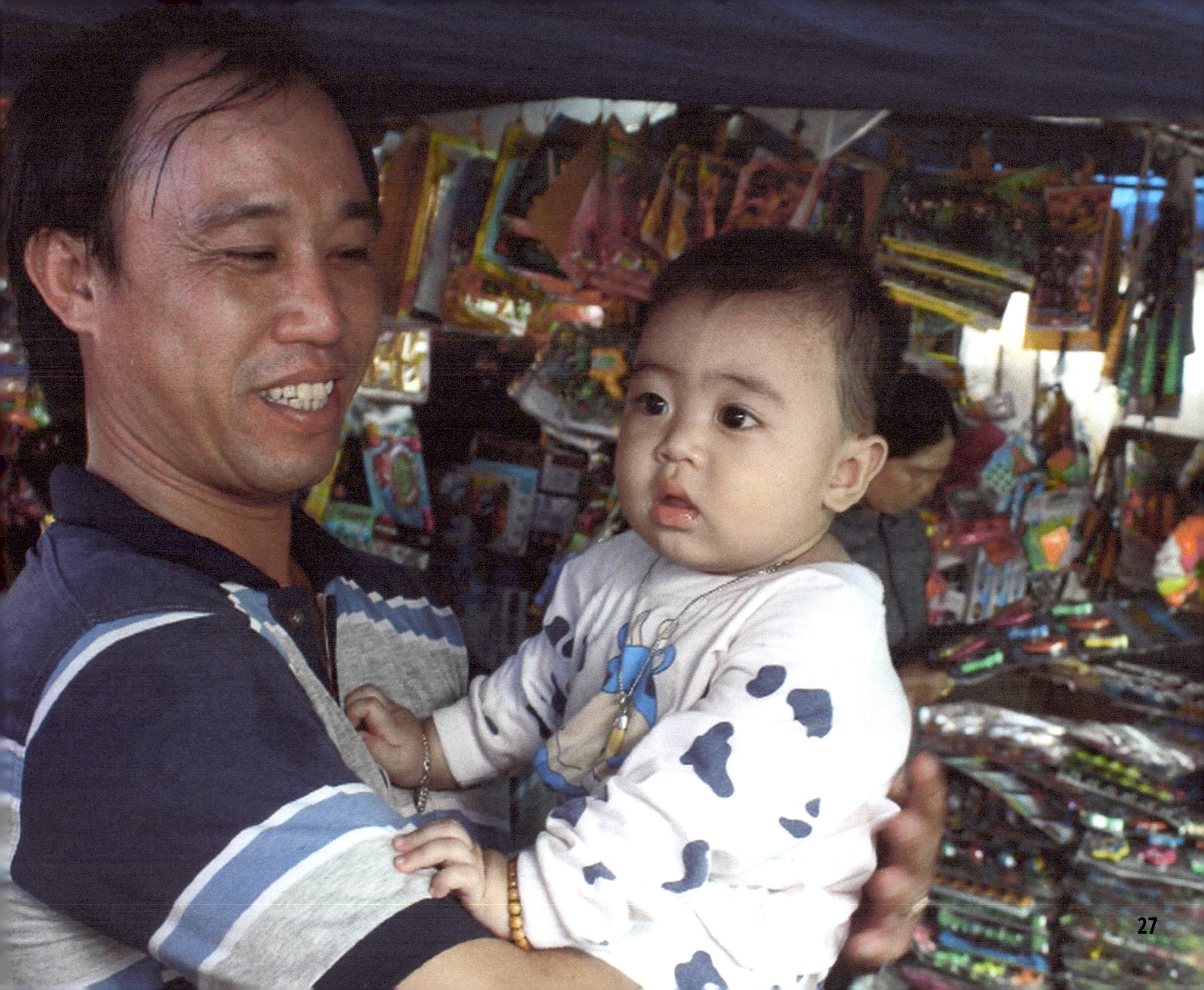

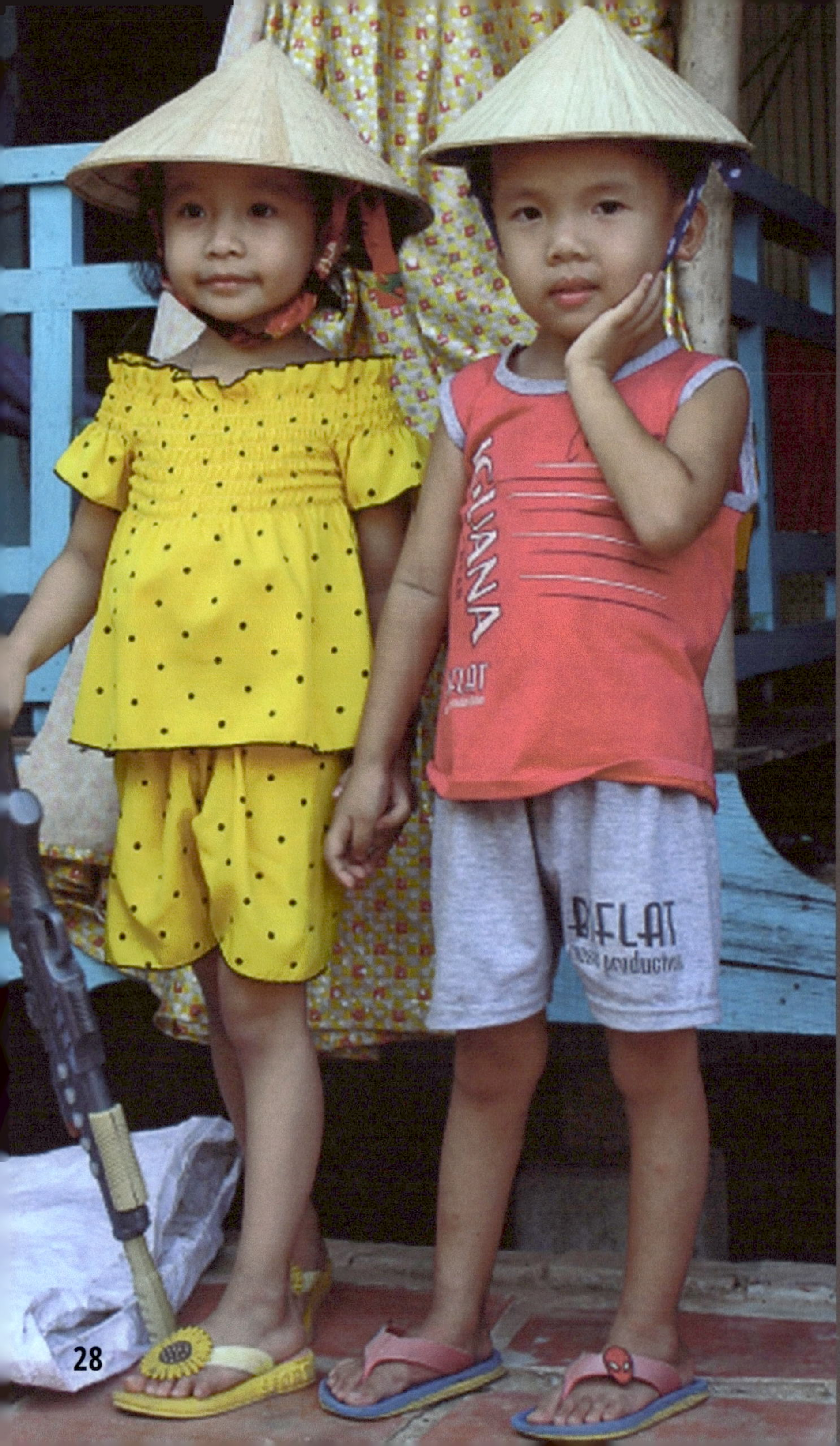

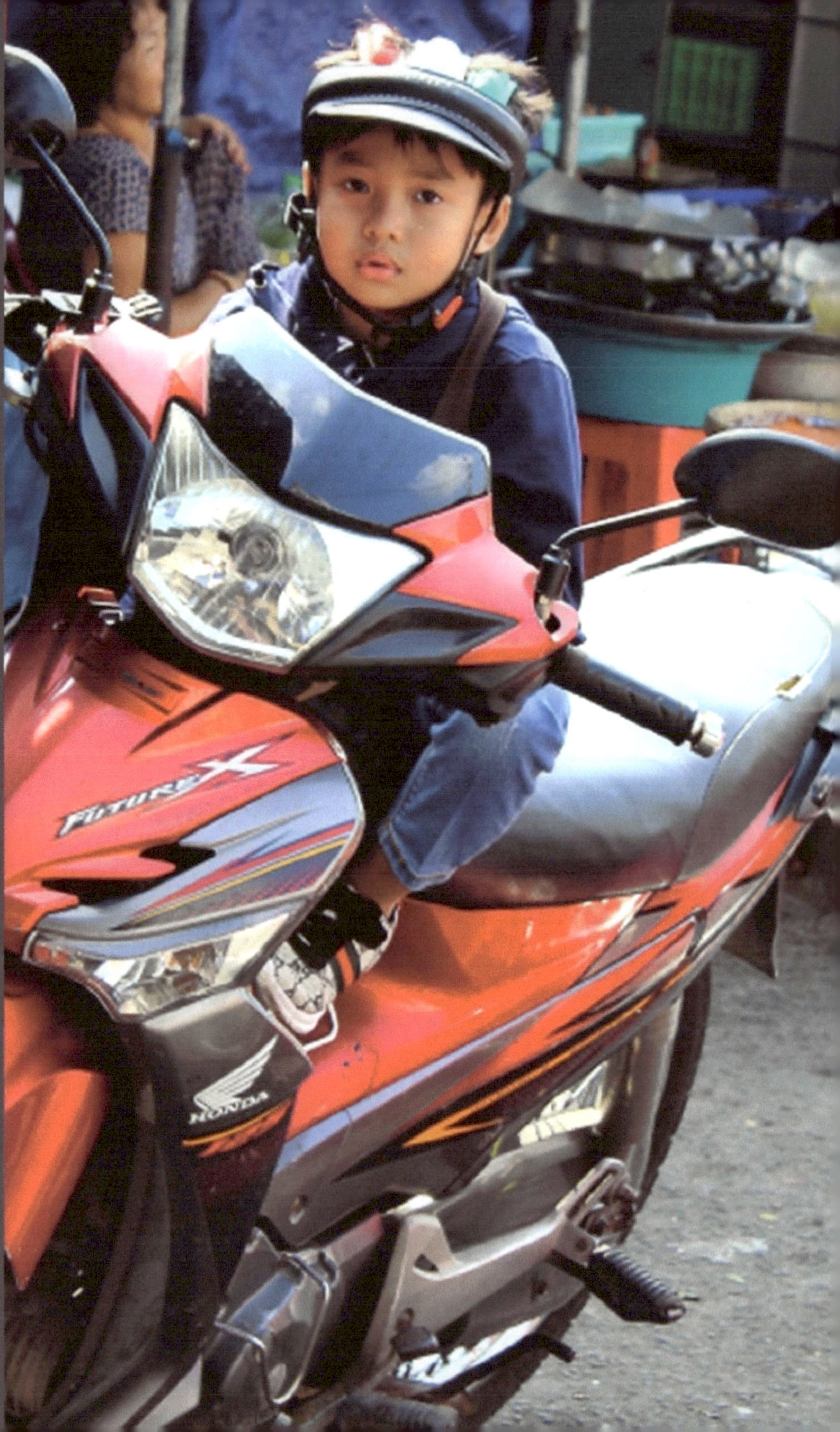

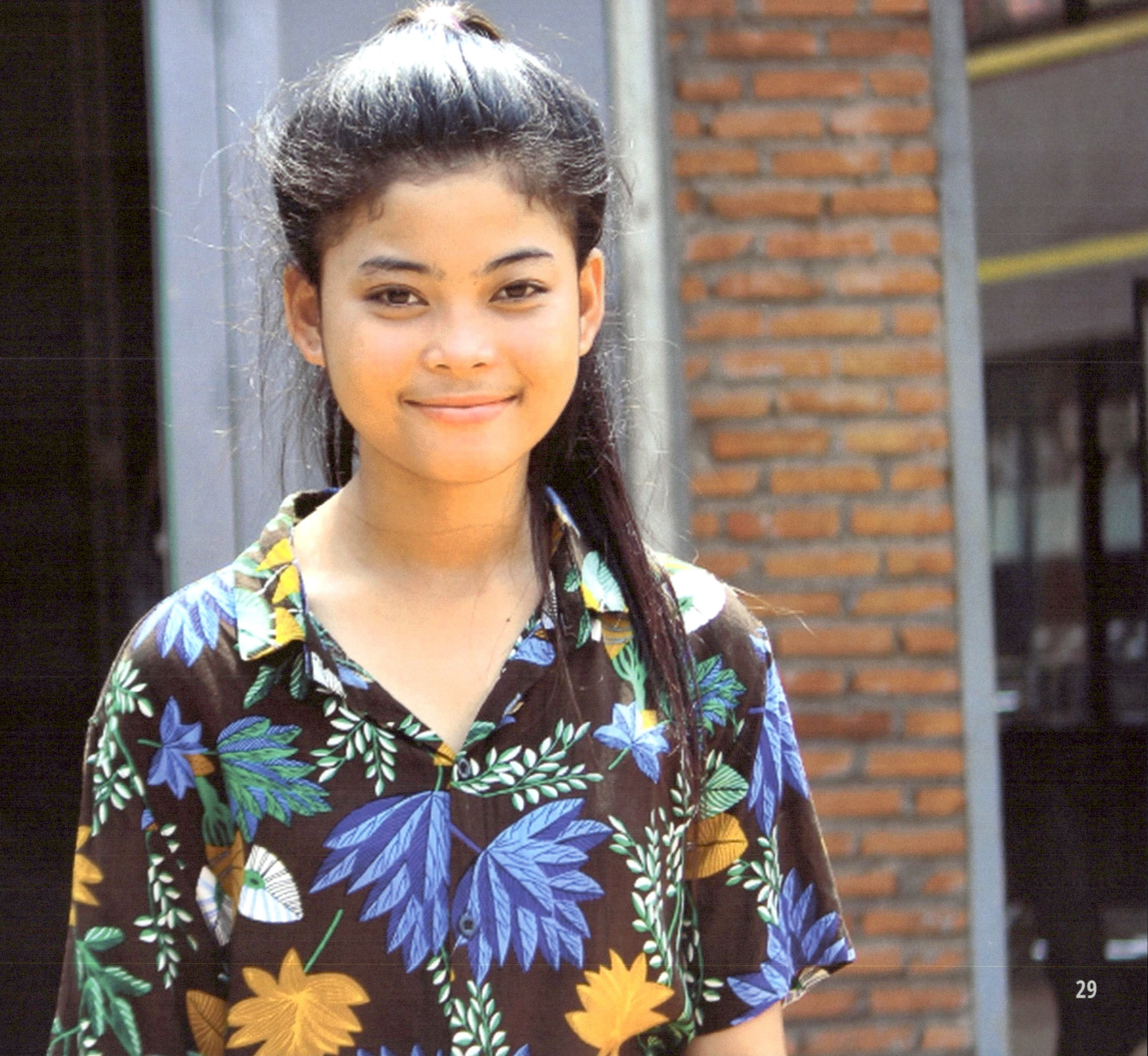

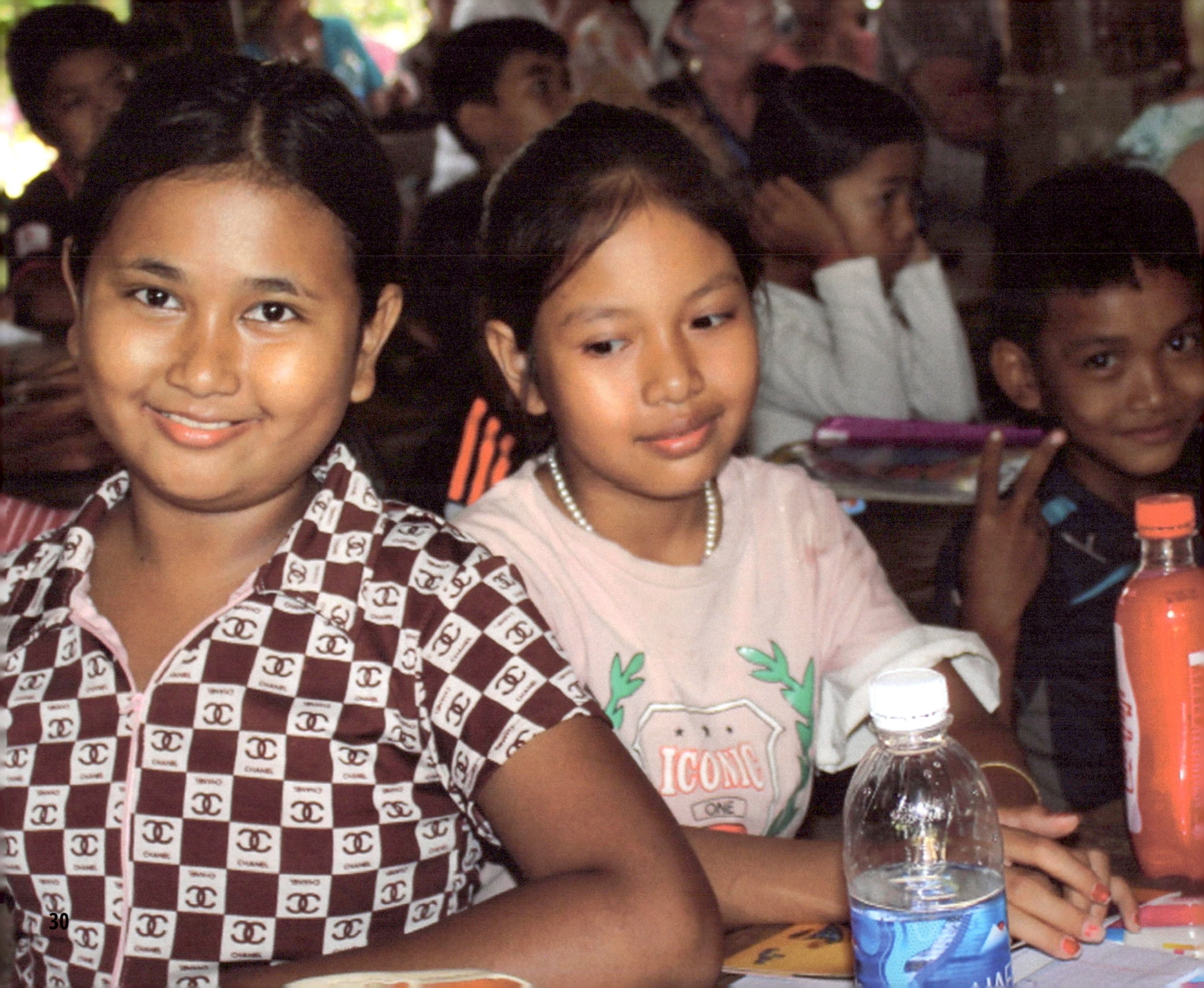

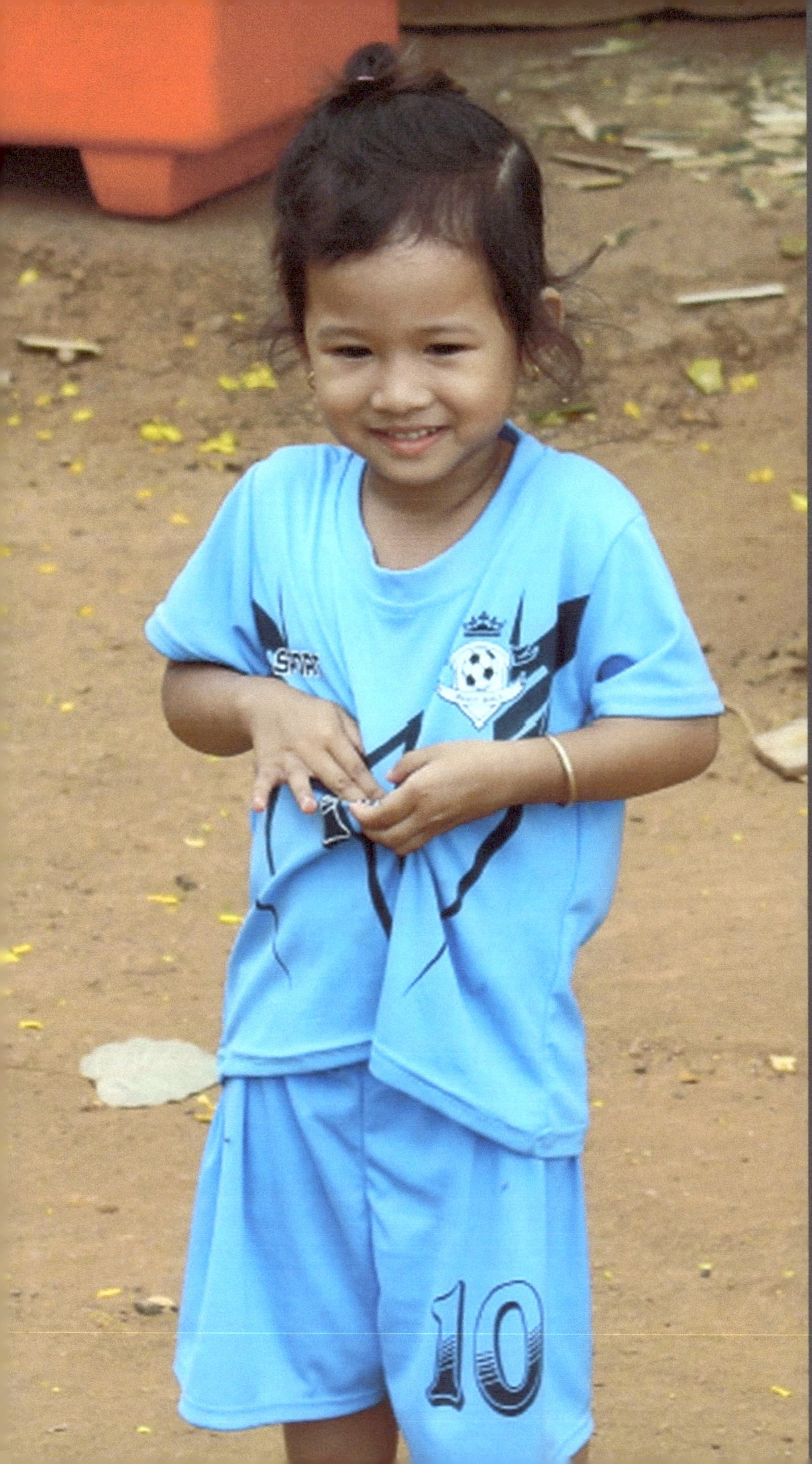

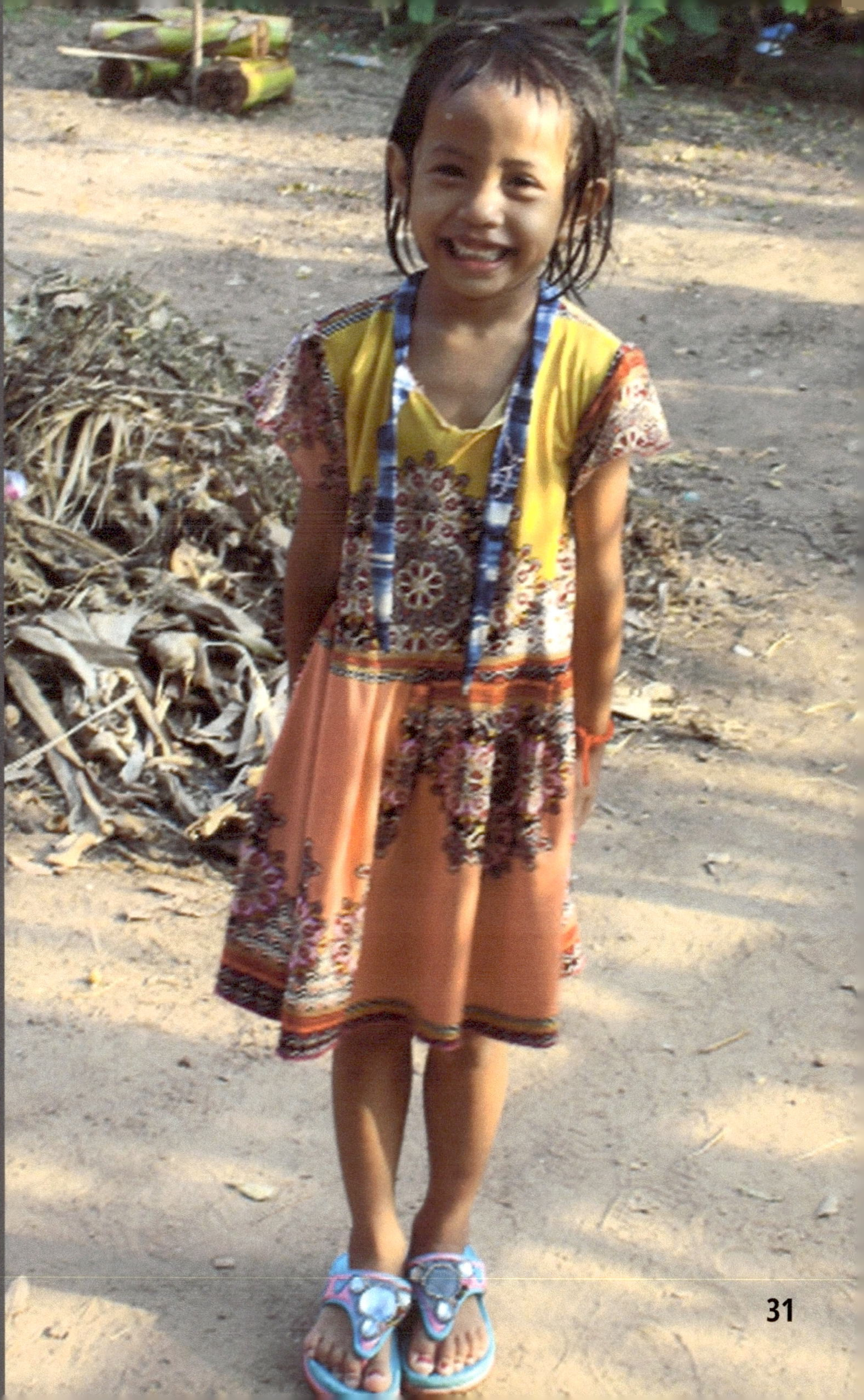

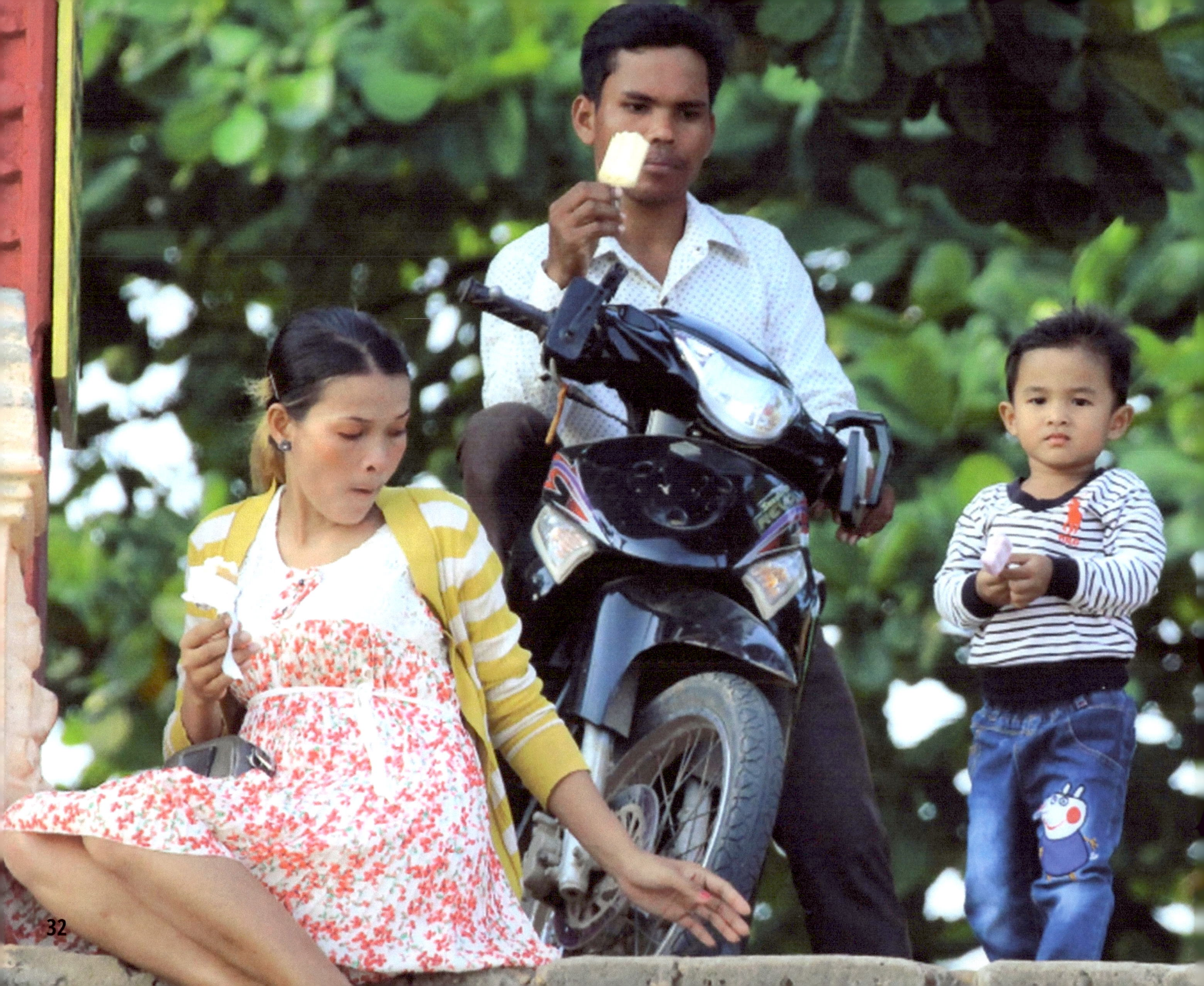

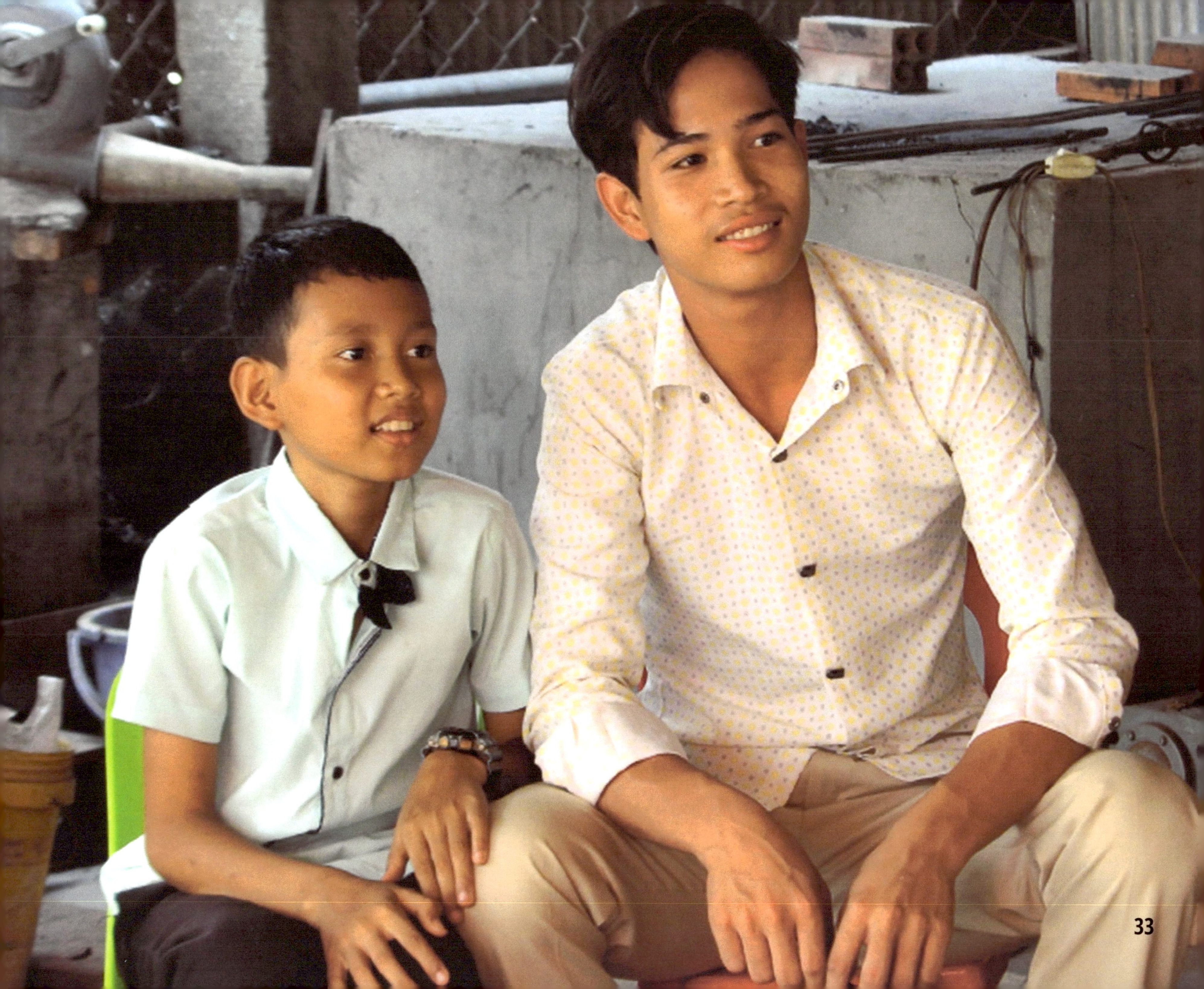

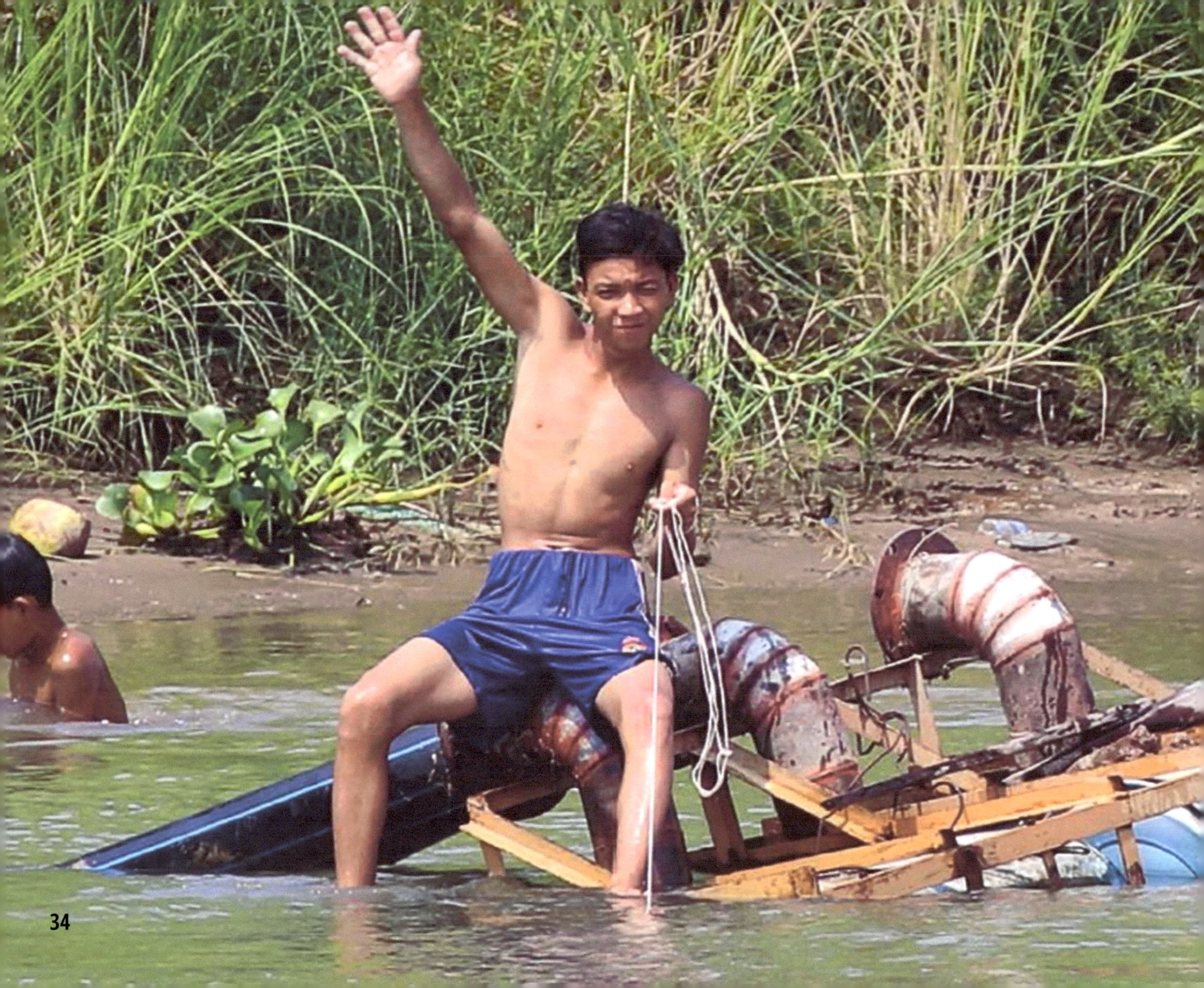

Thomas Auer is a retired family physician who spent 23 years on active duty with the Army Medical Corps. His highly decorated and distinguished career took him to assignments in Wuerzburg, Germany, Ft. Lewis, Wa, Ft. Leonardwood, MO, the Army War College, Washington, DC, and Ft. Bragg, NC. He retired as a Colonel after serving as the Commander of Womack Army Medical Center, Ft. Bragg. His awards include the Legion of Merit and the Meritorious Service Medal each with two Oak Leaf Clusters, and the Order of Military Medical Merit.

His civilian career was just as distinguished and spanned 20 years of leadership positions in private medical groups culminating as the CEO of the Bon Secours Virginia Medical Group in Richmond, VA. He is an avid photographer, traveler, cross country skier, and golfer.

He has been married to Patricia Auer for 49 tremendous years and they have two amazing children, Jeff and Alexis, and their spouses, Amaka and Dave, and two fantastic granddaughters, Erica and Adannaya.

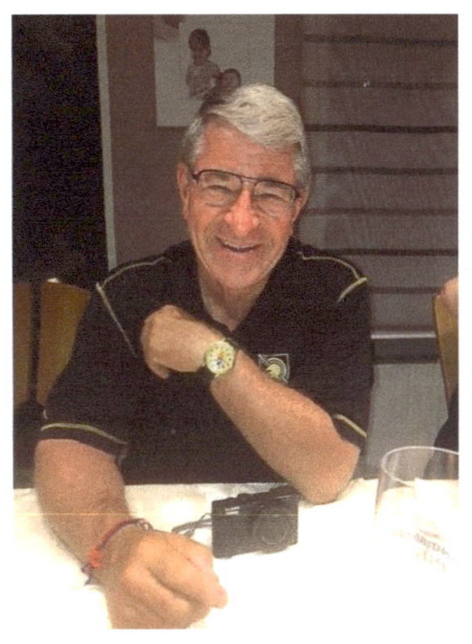